Tourism and Experiential Marketing

Principles, Case Studies, Experiential Quality Seal, Skills and Professional Profiles

Ignazio Caloggero

Cover image: The great attraction of Cappadocia – Credits: iStock.com/Elena-studio

All images, unless otherwise indicated, are by Ignazio Caloggero or come from the site https://www.itinerariesperienziali.it/en/ owned by the Helios Study Center, publisher of this book.

ISBN: 9788832060287

4.2 Quality Factors and Indicators 208
4.3 Factors and Indicators of Experiential Quality 221
4.4 Evaluation of the Quality of the Experiential Offers 225
4.5. Experiential Quality Seal ® 234
5. The Experiential Professions 235
5.1 The recognition of Experience Professionals in Italy 235
5.2 Tourism, Arts, Heritage Competence Framework 238
5.2.1 Training Standards and Professional Standards 238
5.2.2 The Tourism, Arts, Heritage Competence Framework (TAH-CF) 240
5.3 The Professionals of Experiential Experiences 243
5.3.1 Experiential Offerings Specialist 244
5.3.2 Experience Manager 246
5.3.3 Experiential Consultant 248
5.3.4 Experiential Tourism Manager 250
5.3.5 Cultural Heritage Interpreter 254
6. Multimedia Archives of Experiences 258
6.1 Web 3.0 Databases 258
6.2 The Multimedia Experience Database 261
Useful bibliography 262

Premise

Benedetto Croce allegedly stated the following: «Art is what everyone knows what it is.».

Paraphrasing Croce, we could say that the *Experiential Tourism is what everyone knows what it is*, but an all-encompassing definition leaves room for all interpretations, even convenient ones, which would allow the term *Experiential Tourism* to be used as a simple label to stick on as needed, perhaps to justify the prices of their offers.

Therefore, in light of the often uncontrolled and unregulated diffusion of the phenomenon that sees "tourist offers" in the foreground, it becomes useful to identify the elements that distinguish a true experiential offer from a simple tourist offer that only bears the label of experiential. This is fundamental, not only for the tourist, who must choose from an infinite number of available offers, but also for tour operators who aim to provide an authentic and quality tourist experience. Consequently, by applying the Quality Management methodology, the need to provide a clear and unambiguous answer to the following questions emerges:

1. What is Experiential Tourism?
2. What are the characteristics that identify the experiential offer?
3. To what types of activities can experiential principles be applied?
4. How to evaluate the quality of experiential offers?
5. What professional skills are needed?

This book aims to provide concrete answers to the five fundamental questions, focusing on the following aspects, each of which answers the questions formulated above:

1. **Definitions**
2. **Experiential Principles**
3. **Repertoire of experiential activities**
4. **Experiential Quality Mark**
5. **Experiential skills and professional profiles**

The book is mainly aimed at students attending Experiential Tourism courses; however, I believe that it can extend its usefulness to a wider audience, including professionals and operators not only in the tourism area, but also in the commercial one. It is important to underline that, while some concepts, principles and definitions relating to the world of experiences have been revisited or introduced for the first time, this volume probably represents one of the first contributions aimed at integrating experiential principles with Quality Management methodologies.

One of the innovative peculiarities of this volume is its nature as an 'expandable book'. In fact, it offers the possibility of enriching the information present in the text with further details and insights, including multimedia files, which are not included directly in the book. At various points, links and related QR-Codes are provided, leading you towards in-depth information sheets accessible with a phone equipped with a QR-Code reader. I strongly invite you to explore the links, which refer to hundreds of operational examples and real case studies, since, as is well known, images can express more than words; I would also add that videos can express even more than images. The latter can only be viewed by accessing the web pages, which lead to detailed sheets or in-depth videos. The decision to exclude images (and, for obvious reasons, videos) from the book prevented a volume of around 300 pages from swelling to over a thousand pages, with all the related complications that this would have entailed for the paper publication of the book itself, including its costs.

Introduction

As described in its premise, the book aims to give a timely answer to the following five questions:

1. **What is Experiential Tourism?**
2. **What are the defining characteristics of an Experiential Offering?**
3. **To what types of activities can experiential principles be applied?**
4. **How to evaluate the quality of the Experiential Offerings?**
5. **What professional skills are required?**

The initial chapter aims to answer the first question that has been formulated in the introduction:

1. **What is Experiential Tourism?**

To do so, it illustrates the transition from a product-centered economy to an experience economy, as predicted in 1999 by the Americans Pine and Gilmore. The concept of *experience* is then explored, describing the main experiential models and areas, and providing various definitions, including that of *Experiential Tourism* itself. The chapter continues by outlining the ten fundamental principles of experiential offerings, identifying various levels of experience in relation to the application of these principles, and describing a specific experiential model: the theatrical performance. Paragraphs 1.6 and 1.7 explore two key concepts that underlie many experiences: Gastrophysics and the Atmosphere.

Focusing on the second question posed in the introduction, Chapter 2 dives into a detailed discussion on:

2. **What are the defining characteristics of an Experiential Offering?**

This is done by exploring the meaning of the ten principles of the *Experiential Path* in depth, enriching them through practical examples and concrete case studies.

Chapter 3, on the other hand, identifies the various types of activities to which experiential principles can be applied, thus outlining the scope of application of

Experiential Offerings. What emerges in this case is also what I have called *Repertoire of Experiential Activities*, which can be perceived as a classification of the experiential activities themselves. Therefore, the third chapter is dedicated to answering the third question formulated in the introduction:

3. **To what types of activities can experiential principles be applied?**

Each activity is described comprehensively, with the addition of practical examples and real case studies to provide a complete picture.

4. **How to evaluate the quality of the Experiential Offerings?**

The fourth chapter deals with the concept of quality applied to experiences. Among my work experiences, I can include over twenty years dedicated to Quality Management as an Inspector for ISO 9001 certification: it is natural that this professional background influenced my studies in the field of Tourism and Heritage Interpretation, hence the need to connect the entire discussion to the same definition of quality:

It is the ability of a set of characteristics, which are inherent to an ***entity****, to confirm the* ***expectations*** *referable to it by all the* ***parts involved****.*

Once we have defined what quality is, it must be measured, but to do this it is necessary to equip ourselves with an appropriate quality detection system, which leads to the identification of the **entity** to which the concept of quality must be applied by the **parts involved**. These are represented by those who express the expectations or needs according to the entity. There are also **quality factors** to consider.

Quality, once evaluated, must be recognized: here is a paragraph that describes the Experiential Quality Mark created by the Helios Study Center.

5. **What professional skills are required?**

The fifth chapter concerns the recognition of professionals operating in the experiential area. The high specialization and formal recognition of the skills of the professionals involved in the Experiential Transition are of vital importance. When the relevant country allows it, it is crucial that such recognition complies with a national law. In Italy, this is possible thanks to law 4/2013. For other nations, it is essential to examine the existence of specific laws. It is important to underline that the formal recognition of professional skills in a country often enables professionals to operate even in countries that do not have specific laws.

Experiential professionals who aspire to work as Tourism Professionals or Cultural Operators, for whom there is no specific Register, can benefit from the opportunities offered by Law 4/2013 and the Prime Ministerial Decree 14/10/2021, published in the Official Gazette 268 of 10/ 11/2021. It is worthy of note that the Prime Ministerial Decree of 14/10/2021 equates non-professional professions to professional professions for the purposes of employment in the Public Administration. In fact, according to Article 1 of the decree, by *professional* we mean not only those who are registered in professional registers, colleges or orders and those who hold a UNI certification, but also the professionals in possession of the quality and qualification certificate professional services, pursuant to art. 7 of law 14 January 2013, n. 4, issued by a professional association included in the list of the Ministry of Economic Development (now known as the Ministry of Business and Made in Italy).

In the same chapter you can find a reference scheme containing the skills of the Cultural Heritage Interpreter, processed in accordance with the standard: SP/TAH-CF: **Professional Standard (SP)**, based on the professional skills indicated in the reference Framework of skills required and applied in the Tourism, Arts and Cultural Heritage area.

In the sixth and final chapter, the presentation of the Multimedia Archives of Experiences is revealed, which are based on web 3.0 technology, and interconnected with each other.

1. The Experiences

1.1 From Product to Experiences

Experiences often constitute real economic offers aimed at end users, who can be called customers, tourists, guests, or simply users of the experience. Considering this, it is appropriate to review some aspects and changes that affect the very concept of *economic offer*.

Economic offers

The Americans Pine and Gilmore [The Economy of Experience: Beyond Service -1999-2013] distinguish several economic offers:

- **Raw materials** (commodity): fungible materials extracted from the natural, animal, mineral or vegetable world.
- **Goods**: tangible artifacts.
- **Services**: intangible assets.
- **Experiences**: memorable events that involve individuals on a personal level.

Experiences have always been there, but in fact they have been considered within the services. Pine and Gilmore identify economic distinctions based on the type of offer.

Economic Offer	Commodities	Goods	Services	Experiences	Transformations
Economy	Agricultural	Industrial	Service related	Experience related	Transformation related
Economic Function	To Extract	To Build	To Supply	To Stage	To Lead
Nature of the Offer	Fungible	Tangible	Intangible	Memorable	Effective
Key Feature	Natural	Standardized	Customized	Personal	Individual
Supply Method	Mass Supply	Stock-up after Production	On Demand Supply	Revealed after a certain time	Long-lasting
Seller	Merchant	Manufacturer	Supplier	Organizer	Producer
Buyer	Market	User	Customer	Guest	Aspiring
Demand Influences	Features	Aspects	Benefits	Sensations	Traits

Pine and Gilmore underline the fact that over time we have moved from an economy based mainly on raw materials to an economy first based on goods, and subsequently on services. They also state that during the 21st century we will witness the transformation from an economy predominantly based on services to an experience-based economy.

Here are some examples of themed bars and restaurants, where food is just a pretext for what is called "eatertainment" (eat plus entertainment):

Hard Rock Cafe, New York City Tourist Attraction

https://youtu.be/0bTAwJ2pLRM

Discover The Rainforest Cafe | Disneyland Resort Food

https://youtu.be/LqO-Bs5QUQU

Bubba Gump Shrimp Company - Universal Orlando Resort | Forrest Gump Themed Family Restaurant

https://youtu.be/NtDdnbE3i48

Medieval Times - Caneva - Lago di Garda

https://youtu.be/SZmLvXnplZI

In the cases of shops and department stores we instead speak of "shoppertainment" (shopping plus entertainment):

Jordan's Furniture Store Experience

https://youtu.be/F7BZIBHMD5k

NIKETOWN Total Runner's Experience

https://youtu.be/_DRZAHcZpmE

The Memphis Pyramid | Bass Pro Shops

https://youtu.be/1aF4-8tgPWU

Services

Let's remember the definition of service from the point of view of a company:

Service: *Output of an organization with at least one activity necessarily carried out at the interface between the organization and the customer.*

The difference between the services is that the delivery or use of tangible products constitutes only the ancillary tool to what must be considered the primary objective: providing a *performance* to the customer/user/citizen.

Characteristics of the service

Services differ from goods in the following aspects:

- **Intangibility:** The product is generally concrete, while the service is an intangible asset.

For example, a mobile phone is a tangible product; I can touch it without buying it, observe it, and in some cases try it; a specialist visit is not tangible even if it may involve the delivery of a tangible product, such as the document on which the diagnosis is reported.

- **Storage:** The product can be stored, the service cannot.

The mobile phone, once produced, can be stored waiting to be marketed and sold to the final buyer; the specialist view is not a pre-packaged product waiting to be delivered to the user.

- **Heterogeneity:** Unlike the manufacturing area, in services it is difficult to standardize activities, as performance depends on many factors (emotional, behavioral aspects, etc.)

Simply think that a service is provided to people by people, and the countless behavioral differences in each of us.

- **Inseparability**: In products, production and consumption occur in separate places and times; in services, production, provision, and consumption activities by the customer often occur simultaneously.
- **Customer:** The importance of the customer/user/participant is greater as he has an active role right from the production phase of the service.

Experiences

Experiences are a new type of offer. As Pine and Gilmore state:

> *Businesses create experiences when they engage customers in a memorable way.*

If goods (products) are tangible and services are intangible, what characterizes experiences is that they are memorable. In the case of experiences, customers are often referred to as *guests*. Guests value being involved in something personal and memorable.

The transition from a service economy to an experience economy will force many producers to experience their goods; if this is sometimes simple (car manufacturers can always focus on the concept of the driving experience), sometimes it is a little less so: the bolt manufacturer will have some difficulties and will have to appeal to ingenuity.

However, there are various possibilities that each manufacturer can put into practice to offer experiences, for example using an experiential brand for their products (as Nike and Coca Cola do), staging experiential events for their products, creating marketing campaigns that touch the senses and the hearts of its customers, thus relying on what is called Experiential Marketing.

Experiential marketing offers an approach that is focused not so much on the product, but on the consumer, and more precisely on his experiences.

The objective of the strategies of this type of marketing is to identify what type of experience will best enhance the company's goods and services.

1.2 The concept of *experience*

Let's look at some definitions:

Experience: from Latin, *experientia*, derivation of *experiri*, which means 'to try, to experiment'.

- Direct knowledge, personally acquired through observation, use or practice, of a specific sphere of reality.
- In philosophical language, the type of knowledge provided by sensations, or in any case acquired through the senses.
- Knowledge of practical reality considered as a whole.
- Content of human knowledge considered from the point of view of the psychological and cultural changes that it determines in the spiritual development of a person.
- In scientific language, the proof of a principle, a theory, a law, obtained mostly in the laboratory by reproducing a phenomenon to show the dependency relationships between causes and effects.
- In a more general sense, *to experiment*, *to try*.

(Treccani)

Experience: Series of events which mark a person (Sabatini & Coletti, Dictionary of the Italian Language).

Experience: Practical knowledge of life or a certain sphere of reality, acquired with the time and the exercise [...] act or event, occasional or deliberately sought, in which one participated and from which one gained knowledge, modification behavior, sensitivity, etc. (Garzanti linguistics)

Experience: private events that occur in response to some stimulation which, in the business environment, can be constituted by pre-and post-purchase marketing initiatives. Experiences involve the human being as a whole and often result from direct observation or participation in events, whether they are real, fantastic or virtual. [Bernd H. Schmitt, Experiential Marketing 1999]

Experiences: memorable events that involve individuals on a personal level [Pine and Gilmore – 1999]

According to Pine and Gilmore [The Experience Economy: Beyond Service -1999-2013], experiences are personal, they take place within the individual who is involved on an emotional, physical, intellectual or even spiritual level.

The concept of experience is applied to many areas; in the economic field it is considered a category of offer, and we often talk about:

- **Experiential marketing:** when the experience is necessary to the provision of services or sale of products (I don't just sell you the product, but also the experience that comes from it). In practice, companies become suppliers of emotions and experiences.
- **Sensory marketing** (or sensorial branding): falls within experiential marketing; in this case, the objective is to link the sale of a product/service that is being offered, to a multisensory experience in which most of the senses are involved: sight, hearing, touch, taste and smell.
- **Olfactory Marketing**: falls within Sensory Marketing; in this case, the objective is to link the sale of a product/service that is being offered, to one of the five senses, smell.
- **Experiential offer**: when the experience itself is the subject of an offer.

The ultimate objective of sensorial and olfactory marketing is to seduce the customer from an emotional point of view, stimulating memories and positive mental sensations that leads one to buy or create a positive mental image that lasts over time. This happens in order to build customer loyalty.

A restaurant, an accommodation facility, a wellness center, but also a simple point of sale that has had the ability to intelligently dose music, adequate lights, and particular fragrances, will have a high probability of retaining its customers.

In some cases, we witness experiences which, although born as an accessory tool for the sale of goods and services (Experiential Marketing), take on a tourist appeal precisely due to their emotional value.

Offer and Experiential Tourism

For some years now, what is called *Experiential Tourism* has been establishing itself. We are witnessing a cultural evolution of what concerns tourist use. We move from a tourist package, where the tourist has the role of a (passive) spectator, to an offer where the tourist becomes the main (active) actor of the same offer. In new forms of tourism, the tourist package, sometimes understood as a set of tourist services (welcome, accommodation, catering, entertainment, transport, etc.), is essentially made up of the same emotions experienced by the customer. The tourist offer tends to transform itself more and more into a real life (and educational) experience, capable of involving the guest emotionally, intellectually and physically. Essentially, the tourist demand shifts from the classic: «What are you offering me? » to: «What do you make me feel? ».

Experiential offers are certainly capable of making people feel emotions; from an emotional point of view, the definition of *experience* is justified for them. However, it is on the concept of learning, and on other principles that we will see shortly, that they find the true terminological basis, and on which the content of our attempt to provide a formal aspect to the phenomenon of experiential tourism is based.

The bibliography of the related area does not provide a formal and unambiguous definition of experiential tourism; we will try to provide one here, starting from some basic concepts.

Let's start again from Pine and Gilmore's definition:

Experiences: memorable events that involve individuals on a personal level. [Pine and Gilmore – 1999]

Multisensory experiences: Experiences related to multisensory involvement (at least two or more senses: sight, hearing, touch, smell, taste) (Ignazio Caloggero – 2019-2022)

Cultural Experience: Multisensory experiences that allow you to deepen your knowledge of elements of local identity.

Experiential offerings: when the experience is the primary object of the offer.

Experiential Tourism: when the tourist offer includes one or more experiential offerings.

We could say, in general, that every tourist offer can make us feel emotions. We could also theoretically say that every tourist offer makes us learn something. Therefore, we could classify all tourist offers as "experiential offers", as they can involve us on an emotional, physical and intellectual level, or making us learn something (not necessarily in positive terms), but it would only be a way of bringing together experiences that often have little in common.

In some cases, we witness experiences which, although born as an accessory tool for the sale of goods and services (Experiential Marketing), take on a tourist appeal precisely due to their emotional value.

1.3 Models and areas of experiences

Schmitt's experience model

According to the vision of Bernd H. Schmitt [Experiential Marketing 1999], the experience must be considered from a modular point of view: he classifies experiences through 5 strategic experiential modules (SEM, i.e. Strategic Experiential Module).

The 5 types of experience provoked by different stimuli that form the basis of experiential marketing are, according to Schmitt:

- **Sense**
- **Feel**
- **Think**
- **Act**
- **Relate**

Sense: The experience that involves the senses

It appeals to the senses and aims to provide the consumer with a sensorial experience through multi-sensorial involvement: sight, hearing, touch, taste and smell.

Feel: The experience involving feelings and emotions

It recalls consumers' feelings and has the aim of increasing their loyalty, creating an affective experience of the consumer with the company brand. To achieve this objective, the company must be able to arouse moods, emotions and feelings of various nature and intensity in the individual characterized by positivity.

Dior Miss Dior advertisement with Natalie Portman – November 2018

https://youtu.be/9Y_33PAl1XA

SKY Nameless emotions

https://youtu.be/74FgLyQ7wLo

Think: Cognitive experience

It appeals to the intellect and has the goal of creating cognitive and problem-solving experience.

Act: experiences that involve physicality

It pushes the user to live bodily experiences and interact with other individuals. The goal is to enrich the consumer's life by improving their physical experiences and showing them alternative ways of acting.

Experiential Marketing Campaign – Vitamin Water

https://youtu.be/EIdUzGo6BUM

Nike: This is us

https://youtu.be/1OYi2pbNK_4

Relate: the experiences that arise from interactions and relationships with others

It also incorporates the aspects of Sense, Feel, Think and Act. It makes the individual relate to the socio-cultural context, stimulating social relationships that involve the brand. The objective is to create a brand community that sees the company brand as a point of reference.

Harley-Davidson commercial

https://youtu.be/16brzoKerxg

Apple Think different 1997 commercial

https://youtu.be/q4gF1PNhXNE

To activate the modules of Sense, Feel, Think, Act and Relate, the company must resort to tools that are defined as Experience Providers (ExPro):

- Communication
- People
- Websites and multimedia
- The exhibition spaces
- The visual/verbal identity
- The presence of the product.

Pine and Gilmore's domains of experience

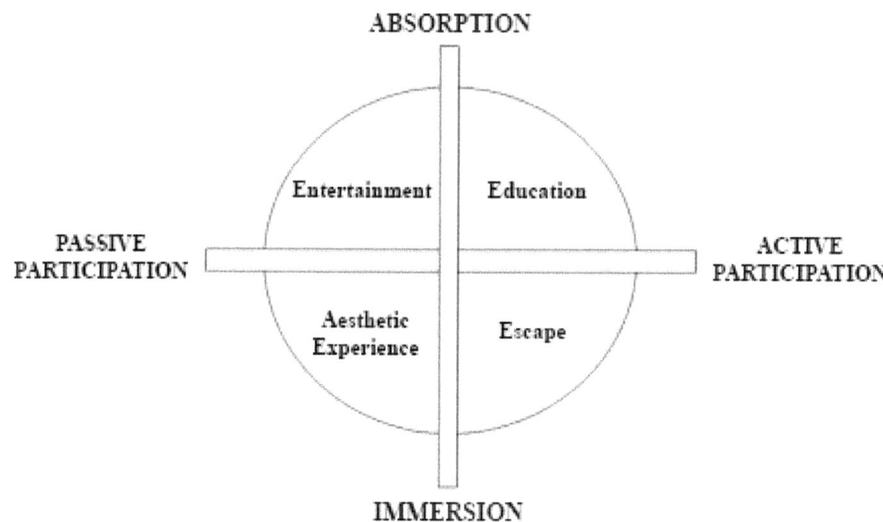

In the model of Pine and Gilmore, four domains of experience are identified:

The first dimension (along the horizontal axis) of the experience areas corresponds to the level of participation of the guests: we start from a **passive participation**, in which the customers do not act or influence the performance directly (e.g. concert goers of classical music, who live the experience as simple listeners) up to an **active participation**, in which customers personally act on the performance or event that produces the experience (e.g. participants in the various forms of tourism adventure, including hiking).

The second dimension (along the vertical axis) describes the type of connection or environmental relationship that unites customers with the event, or performance, represented. We start from **Absorption**, where the experience *penetrates* the person through the mind (e.g. when watching a film on TV) up to **Immersion**, in which the person "enters into" the experience, physically or virtually part of the same (e.g. watching a film at the cinema with tools that increase virtual reality).

The union of these dimensions defines the four domains of an experience:

- Entertainment
- Education
- Evasion
- Aesthetic experience

These areas are mixed to different extents and proportions, depending on the type of experience and the guest involved, helping to create unique, personal and unrepeatable events.

The degree of customer involvement depends both on the customer itself (level of predisposition to be involved in a given event) and on the organization offering the experience (ability to involve customers).

- **The scope of entertainment**: it occurs when people passively absorb events through one or more senses, as it usually happens when listening to music, watching a film, or reading for pleasure.
- **The scope of education**: Even in educational experiences, people absorb events, but unlike entertainment, education involves the active participation of the individual.
- **The scope of aesthetic experience**: in these forms of experiences individuals immerse themselves in an event or environment but remain passive. Typical aesthetic experiences are touristic ones, such as visiting a natural park, an art gallery or a museum. The aesthetics of an experience can be completely natural (e.g. natural park), essentially artificial (e.g. theme park), or an intermediate reality. It should be clarified that the experience itself is not artificial: every experience created in the individual is real, regardless of whether it is based on a natural or artificial event.
- **The scope of the escape**: Escapist experiences involve immersion in the event and active participation. Compared to purely entertainment or educational experiences, the guest in this case is completely immersed in them, just like

aesthetic experiences, but thanks to his active participation the user becomes a protagonist of the event that constitutes the experience. An example of escape can be found in any adventure tourism offers (excursions) or direct participation in extreme sports (kayaking).

By participating in an **aesthetic** experience, guests will want to **be there**; they will want to **watch** something during an experience of **entertainment**; to **try** during an experience of **escapism**; to **learn** during an **educational** experience. [Pine and Gilmore: The Experience Economy 1999]

The richest and most engaging experiences include aspects of all four domains.

«When all four domains are in the same setting, then and only then does the space become a special place to stage an experience.» [Pine and Gilmore: The Experience Economy 1999]

1.4 The Principles of the Experiential Path

In the remainder of the discussion, the term *path* will be often used, preferring it to *offer*, to underline the fact that a path is a set of activities linked together, which aim at a very specific purpose, but which do not necessarily have to be configured as a tourist offering.

To be truly considered such, an experiential path should respect a series of principles that define it:

- **Multisensoriality**: The experiential path must include multisensory activities (involvement of the senses: sight, hearing, touch, smell and, where possible, taste).
- **Local identities**: The experiential path must allow to deepen the knowledge of elements of local identity.
- **Uniqueness**: the experiential path must present unique characteristics.
- **Human relationships**: the experiential path must be based on human relationships.
- **Direct participation**: the experiential path must provide for the direct participation of the guest in some activities.
- **Experiential learning**: the experiential path must include a learning phase through the direct participation of the guest in some activities.
- **Thematic approach**: each path must be built starting from a theme that characterizes it and which constitutes its guiding thread.
- **Aesthetic approach**: The aesthetic approach is one of the elements, together with that of direct participation, at the basis of the concept of *immersion*. The events that constitute 'the staging of the experience' must be designed in such a way as to give importance to all aspects that can influence aesthetics: the atmosphere, the sense of beauty, the place chosen for the experience, the plot (screenplay) which must be consistent with the chosen theme and the identified location.
- **Entertainment**: the experiential journey should also include moments of entertainment, which enrich and make the experience pleasant.
- **Immersion**: The principle of immersion is the direct consequence of the application of the principles of multisensory, direct participation and aesthetic

approach. Immersive techniques can be implemented to create a scenic environment that sees participants immersed in a multisensory context.

Experience levels are linked at the level of application of these principles.

Experiences (mainly commercial):

- **Experience (First Level):** Multisensory experience, which presents unique characteristics (principles 1, 3).
- **Authentic Experience (Second Level):** Multisensory, unique experience, based on human relationships, which involve the direct participation of guests, and based on a thematic approach (principles 1, 3, 4, 5, 7).
- **Full Experience (Third Level):** Multisensory, unique, thematic and immersive experience, based on human relationships, which involves the direct participation of guests in the activities that constitute the experience itself (principles 1, 3, 4, 5, 7, 8, 9, 10).

Cultural experiences

- **Cultural Experience (First Level):** Multisensory experience that allows you to deepen your knowledge of elements of local identity (principles 1, 2, 3).
- **Authentic Cultural Experience (Second Level):** Multisensory, unique experience, based on human relationships, which allows the understanding of elements of local identity through direct participation in the activities that constitute the experience itself (principles 1, 2, 3, 4,5, 6, 7, XNUMX).
- **Full Cultural Experience (Third Level):** Multisensory, unique, thematic and immersive experience, based on human relationships, which allows the understanding of elements of local identity through direct participation in the activities that constitute the experience itself (principles 1, 2, 3, 4, 5, 6, 7, 8, 9, 10).

Unlike what I have done in the past, I wanted to distinguish predominantly commercial experiences from purely cultural ones, depending or not on the involvement, in the offer, of aspects relating to local identities (Cultural Heritage).

Endogenous and exogenous experiential principles

Another aspect to take into consideration relates to the endogenous or exogenous applicability of the principle, based on the type of experiential activity:

- **Endogenous principle:** the principle is respected by the very nature of the experiential offerings.
- **Exogenous principle:** the principle is respected by integrating elements that enrich the experience.

Let's take for example the principle of **multisensoriality**.

A walk in the fields, in close contact with nature or in places of production in a rural environment, can be an opportunity for a truly unique multisensory experience (endogenous requirement):

- **Touch**: perceive the effects of the wind on the skin and touch flowers, animals, trees with your hands.
- **Hearing:** the sound of insects, animals or the noises of nature.
- **Smell:** the smell of flowers, hay, crushed grapes, wine, pressed oil, aromatic herbs.
- **Sight:** the vision of natural, cultural beauties or animals encountered, or foods tasted.

The multisensory requirement can also be applied in other contexts exogenously by simply adding, where necessary, elements that enrich the experience: shine, herbs, sounds, immersive environments, and other sensory stimuli.

The macro-objectives of the experiential process

Below is a subdivision of the principles of the experiential path (in brackets), based on what we can consider the macro-objectives of the experiential process:

- **Experiences through the senses** (sensory involvement) (1, 5, 7, 8, 10)
- **Experiences through emotions** (emotional involvement) (2, 3, 4, 6, 9)

The principles should not be seen as belonging strictly to one of the macro-objectives mentioned, as each principle can constitute a strengthening element of other principles included in other macro-objectives. Even the two macro-objectives presented should not be seen independently, in fact, for example, sensory involvement is also an essential element for emotional involvement.

Experiences through the senses (sensory involvement)

The principles particularly involved, and which contribute to sensorial involvement are:

1) Multisensory approach

5) Participation

7) Thematic approach

8) Aesthetic approach

10) Immersion

The direct experiences and observations carried out in the field are in themselves multisensory (1), as they involve the involvement of most of the senses: sight, hearing, touch, smell and in some cases, taste. The direct participation of guests (5) in activities carried out in an environment carefully curated from an aesthetic point of view (8) will contribute to making the experience immersive (10).

Even a consistent theme (7) that constitutes the underlying theme of the interpretative path will contribute to the principle of immersion, and therefore to sensorial involvement.

Experiences through emotions (emotional involvement)

Remembering that sensorial involvement is also an essential element for emotional involvement, the other principles that are particularly relevant and which contribute, together with those listed, to emotional involvement are:

2) Cultural approach (local identities)

3) Uniqueness

4) Relational approach (centrality of the participants)

6) Educational process (experiential learning)

9) Entertainment

The principles Cultural Approach (2) and Uniqueness (3) are endogenous principles in cultural experiential paths and are the basis of the emotional involvement of the participants.

An experiential path, of whatever type it is, should be characterized by the fact that it is an interactive process which translates into a strong relationship between those who offer the experience and those who receive it (4). We are witnessing a form of customization of the experience, also based on the personality of the guest who takes on a central role.

The presence of moments of experiential learning (6) in which the direct participation of the guests is expected, in addition to strengthening the principle of immersion and therefore greater sensorial involvement, also constitutes an element of emotional involvement. This is the case, for example, of experiential courses that include moments of direct learning carried out in production centers (cellars, breweries, oil mills, farms, etc.) and in educational activities in the laboratory or in the field.

The moments of entertainment (9) are certainly useful for the emotional involvement of the participants, especially if there is a direct involvement of the participants in playful and recreational activities linked to aspects considered cultural identities (dancing, playing, singing, etc.).

1.5 Theater as a model of experience

In the conception and planning phase of an experiential path, it can be helpful to use a representative model of the experience: the theatrical show.

Elements underlying the experience seen as a theatrical show are the following:

- **The production (who)**: The organization (or "experience director"), which has the responsibility of designing and staging the experience.
- **The show (what):** the experiential offer which will be characterized by a theme and a plot (screenplay).
- **The actors (with whom):** the staff involved in the experiential offering.
- **The public (for whom):** The guests. When guests are involved through active participation, they will become actors themselves and will contribute to the show.
- **The stage (where):** the location chosen for the experience, which can be a limited physical place, but in some cases can consist of the territory itself.

Elements of staging

Furthermore, when staging the experience, it may be useful to consider the following elements [The Experience Economy: Beyond the Service -1999-2013]:

1. Making it a thematic experience.
2. Inserting positive clues (stimuli) that harmonize impressions.
3. Eliminating negative clues that distract from the topic.
4. Engaging the five senses.
5. Integrating with souvenir objects (keepsakes).

Thematic experience

The theme is the starting point of the experience; it is the common thread that allows you to identify the place, the plot and the most suitable scenography elements to make the experience truly memorable.

If it is a cultural experiential offering, therefore the theme should be in harmony with the territory it belongs to. Some areas of belonging in which to find inspiration for the themes to choose can be the following:

- Culture and traditions.
- Artistic craftsmanship.
- Knowledge and ancient crafts.
- Myths and legends.
- Food & wine.
- Natural aspects characterizing the territory.
- Aspects related to places of memory (historical, literal, filmic events, etc.)

Inserting positive clues (stimuli) that harmonize impressions.

Positive cues that reinforce the experience can be physical or behavioral.

Physical clues are:

- visions
- herbs
- flavors
- sounds

Behavioral clues related to this role:

- Appropriate staff behavior
- Appropriate clothing
- Thematic and appropriate language

Eliminating negative clues that distract from the topic.

The previously described clues can be positive, but also negative: sounds and visions out of context can disturb the experience; also, architectural aspects that are neglected or inconsistent with the theme are to be considered clues that contradict or divert attention from the theme itself, and therefore they disorientate the guest, making the experience less memorable.

Even an excessive number of clues, apparently inserted to improve the content of the experience, can divert attention from the theme: an interlocutor who is too verbose, an excess of scenography content. It is always advisable to keep in mind the ancient saying: 'too much breaks the bag.'

Engaging the five senses.

The more an experience can involve all the senses of a guest, the more it will contribute to an immersive and therefore memorable journey.

Integrating with souvenir objects (keepsakes).

Souvenir objects allow you to extend the experience and constitute a tangible testimony of it. This especially happens if the objects are the result of part of the experience (e.g. small artistic craft objects made on your own during the experience).

Gastrophysics

For some years, the term *gastrophysics* has been used. in the food and wine sector. It was coined by Charles Spence, experimental psychologist and university professor at the University of Oxford, author of the 2017 book "Gastrophysics. The new science of eating", translated and published in Italian in 2020 by Readrink with the title "Gastrophysics. The new science of eating".

In the book, Spence gives the following definition of gastrophysics:

Scientific study of the factors that influence our sensory perception while tasting foods and drinks[1].

The term derives from the union of two words: gastronomy and psychophysics, where the latter identifies the scientific study of perception.

Gastrophysics is the basis of many food and wine experiences. Spence rightly underlines that the discipline does not only apply to luxury foods and drinks, as the study of the factors that influence our senses while we eat and drink can find application in any food and wine context, especially if we want to apply an important principle of experiences, the multisensory one. Gastrophysics concerns the study of the five senses: taste, smell, sight, hearing and touch.

Taste

One of the five senses with which the man is equipped: it is the specific sense exercised through the gustatory organs or taste organs (papillae contained in the various parts of the oral cavity, glossopharyngeal nerve, chorda tympani), through which it is possible to recognize and control the taste of substances introduced into the oral cavity (Treccani).

Taste is therefore the sensation produced when a substance in the mouth reacts chemically with the receptors present on the taste buds.

[1] Charles Spence - Gastrofisica. La nuova scienza del mangiare, p. 22

Five fundamental (or primary) tastes are normally indicated:

- Sweet
- Sour
- Salty
- Bitter
- Umami

The last taste mentioned, Umami (a Japanese term meaning 'delicious taste'), is a taste coming from glutamic acid and often associated with a derivative known as monosodium glutamate; it is present, for example, in tomatoes or parmesan, and is typical of bouillon cubes.

Some researchers suggest including other flavors, including **kokumi**, **metallic** and the **fatty acid**.

The combination of primary tastes generates all the others. Each taste is able, by interacting with the others, to enhance or 'cover' the other tastes.

Furthermore, the perception of taste can also be influenced by other aspects, such as color and smell.

As a rule, it is difficult to feel a single taste alone and distinctly, except cases such as having exaggerated with salt, making the food too salty.

The taste map

For many years it was believed that the taste buds react differently to various tastes depending on their position, and that each taste is recognized by a specific part.

This is not the case: the taste perceivers are distributed uniformly on the tongue; furthermore, the perception of tastes is distributed indifferently across the entire tongue and in other areas of the mouth.

The misconception of the taste map originated from a mistranslation of an article written in 1901 "Zur Psychophysik des Geschmackssinnes" (On the Psychophysics of Taste), which noted small differences in the taste perception threshold in different regions of the tongue. In 1942 the American psychologist **Edwin Boring** translated the text into English: in his version, however, it was not stated that the human tongue has areas of sensitivity relating to tastes, but on the contrary that certain areas only sensed those specific tastes. Other later translations have favored the taste map belief.

One of the frequent mistakes is to consider aspects such as: the burning sensation caused by chili pepper, or the freshness caused by a mint candy, as if they were tastes: they are not, in these cases we should rather talk about flavors.

Flavors

The terms *taste* and *flavor* are often used synonymously, but they do not mean the same thing.

Flavors arise from the combined effect of taste, olfactory processes, and by the chemical activation of receptors for physical stimuli (**chemesthesis**).

Smell is the sense that most influences flavors, as it has a direct connection with the brain.

Food is made up of molecules; with the chewing process, the aroma molecules detach from the food and go up to the nasal cavity (retronasal perception). Here, thousands of receptors detect, analyze odors, then send the information to the brain for processing. The result of this processing is nothing else than the sensation that we call **taste**.

If we try to plug our nose, excluding or in any case reducing the olfactory process, only the taste will remain, as often happens when we have a cold and lose the pleasure of flavor in the foods we eat.

The gustatory experience is therefore multisensory, as Charles Spence recalls: even biting into a fresh apricot turns out to be a multisensory experience, as the brain puts together the scent, the flavor, the consistency, the color, the sound of the teeth sinking into the juicy pulp, not to mention the furry feel of the peel on your hand and inside your mouth[2].

Expectations that influence taste (psycho-taste)

Taste can be influenced by many aspects, in particular by expectations arising from:

- **the price** (if it is expensive, then it must be good).
- **the label** (if pleasant, it favors positive judgement).
- **the brand** (it is believed, not always with good reason, that well-known and famous brands are a guarantee of quality).
- **the color**: it is assumed that some colors make you think of certain tastes: green to mind, pink to fruit, etc.
- **the description:** describing a food in a positive or negative way will create positive and negative expectations, which will influence the final judgment.
- **the memories:** even the memories linked to the food we are tasting will influence the judgment on the taste.
- **the atmosphere:** if pleasant and in harmony with what we are eating, it will positively strengthen the food and wine experience.

Taste and smell

Odors can be perceived in two ways:

- **Orthonasal perception**: odors that reach the nose directly from the external environment.
- **Retronasal perception**: When you eat or drink, aroma molecules, which are light and volatile, leave the food or drink and rise from the back of your mouth to the nasal cavity.

In some cases, background aromas are used (**atmospheric aromas**) to create a particular atmosphere or climate that serves to strengthen the food and wine experience. In this case it is always advisable to be careful so that the background scent does not compete with the aromas of the food itself (**aromas in the foreground**) [3].

[2] Charles Spence - Gastrofisica. La nuova scienza del mangiare, p. 18

Scents can also be used to stimulate memories and positive mental associations.

Sight: Food and colors: *eating with your eyes.*

The visual impact of a food may condition the personal perception of taste. In fact, taste is influenced by what you see while eating. The perception of aromas and flavors is conditioned by the intensity and tone of the colors of the food.

Each color contributes to the transmission of information on edibility, identity and intensity of flavor and taste, leading to choosing certain foods over others.

From a research conducted by Supreet Saluja and Richard J Stevenson in 2018 entitled: "Cross-Modal Associations Between Real Tastes and Colors", it emerges that there would be a certain tendency to ensure that:

- Sweet is represented by pink and red.
- Sour is represented by yellow and green.
- Salty is represented by white and blue.
- Bitter is represented by black and purple.

By applying the reverse reasoning, therefore starting from a color to connect a flavor, the results are slightly different, and not always uniform with each other. In fact, there can be different meanings based on the culture or emotional mental associations of each individual.

---

[3] Charles Spence – Gastrofisica. La nuova scienza del mangiare, p. 99

Generally speaking:

- Red recalls a spicy flavor.
- Green recalls a sour and unripe taste.
- Yellow reminds of a sour taste.
- Blue reminds of an artificial or salty flavor.
- Orange recalls a spicy flavor.
- Pink recalls a sweet taste.
- Purple recalls a sweet taste.
- Brown reminds of a burnt flavor.
- Black recalls a bitter taste.
- White turns out to be tasteless or sweet.

This type of association is sometimes used in the context of **experiential marketing** and for the conception of the **packaging**. Even the shape influences the personal perception of taste, which is why the art of setting the table, as well as the food design, has been spreading more and more for years.

Just like it happens with art, sometimes this discipline is perhaps taken a little too seriously, or there is a shift from a taste for beauty to the one of surprising at all costs.

Hearing

Hearing, and in particular sounds, can influence the food and wine experience. In fact, in addition to having a positive or negative impact on our mood, it can also change the taste of food, even altering its perception.

For example, the sound of the sea can enhance the flavor of oysters, just as some sounds associated with summer could enhance the perceived freshness of strawberries.

Charles Spence, through his research, discovered that certain sounds can affect people's taste buds and that music can make food seem 10% sweeter or saltier.

It should be kept in mind that, during a meal, intense and/or prolonged external auditory stimuli can decrease sensitivity to flavors. In fact, noise not only affects hearing, but also taste.

For example, music and the entire environment often affect guests' own behaviors.

Below are some examples:

- Excessive background music can be a nuisance, as well as sometimes not facilitating simple communication between fellow diners.
- Loud, rhythmic music tends to create an atmosphere that leads to reducing the time spent in a place where you eat or drink: it is in fact used in some places to free up seats sooner.
- Classical music creates a relaxing atmosphere, tends to make people stay longer and make the customer willing to pay more for the service.

Obviously, the type of music must also adapt to the context: it probably won't happen often to hear classical music in a fast-food restaurant or a Bavarian beer hall.

The sounds of preparation

Sounds can constitute:

- **positive stimuli**: they create expectations and improve the perception of flavors. For example, the noise of the coffee grinder (if not too loud and not excessively high in frequency) is a positive stimulus.
- **negative stimuli**: hearing the microwave signaling the end of heating in a luxury restaurant could be seen as a non-positive sound by many diners.

The intrinsic sounds of foods that occur during chewing can also be a positive stimulus, for example the crunch of chips. Indeed, in some cases, such as that of chips, bags are created which contain them in such a way as to produce a certain noise, which recalls the concept of crunchiness.

The sounds of preparation in the kitchen, if well selected, can stimulate and create expectations that favor judgments relating to a food and wine experience. Some chefs offer experiences enriched by the sounds of preparation.

Food Ensemble – Electronic Kitchen

Food Ensemble: they are three young artists who cook live and transform the sounds of preparation into songs to accompany the tasting. The dishes are made before the eyes of the spectator just like in a cooking show, the sounds of preparation are transformed and become live music like in a live concert. The experience consists of a four-course tasting combined with a concert of four compositions. The Ensemble is made up of Francis Sarcone, musician and award-winning sound designer, sound manipulator to compose express music, Andrea Reverberi, chef trained in traditional cuisines, lover of mixing flavors and experiences, and Marco Chiussi, sound engineer, sous-chef and sommelier.

Food Ensemble

https://youtu.be/CewcbMXMr18

The Fat Duck Sound of the Sea

https://youtu.be/R_6vJ4jB0B0

1.7 The Atmosphere

The atmosphere, seen as an aesthetic component of the environment (the sounds, the smells, the shapes of the objects, the dishes, the tables themselves, the guest rooms, the furnishings and even the softness of the chair or sofas on where we sit, as well as the beds), influences the experience that is offered.

The atmosphere can be directly linked to the places in which the structure offering the experience is inserted, or created specifically within any additional events that enrich the primary offer: food and wine events, cultural events, exhibition events, entertainment shows entertainment, additional services offered.

The comfort of the seats also affects the length of stay: comfortable seats tend to make diners stay longer, uncomfortable seats will lead to a reduction in the time spent in the place where you eat or drink.

The atmosphere also affects choices in some way. A group of researchers did an experiment in an English supermarket and discovered that, when playing French music with an accordion, customers bought more bottles of French wine (77% compared to other bottles). The percentage was reduced to 23% if German beer hall music was played. Similarly, the bottles of German wine were 73% if German beer hall music was played, which was reduced to 27% if the music played was French music with the accordion[4].

---

[4] Charles Spence – Gastrofisica. La nuova scienza del mangiare

Ultraviolet restaurant in Shanghai

The restaurant Ultraviolet in Shanghai, created by famous French chef Paul Pairet, is known for offering multisensory, immersive, and atmospheric food and wine experiences. The restaurant can only seat ten people at a time; during the meal, the dining room, which is initially bare and white, is transformed through lights, sounds and scents, creating an atmosphere that changes with each course served. For example, one version of the hall, called *Autumn Soil*, resembles an enchanted forest. The technology used includes lights, projectors, scent diffusers, infrared cameras, and a surround sound system, all controlled remotely from a 'Techno Room'.

https://www.itinerariesperienziali.it/en/directory-offerte/listing/ristorante-ultraviolet-di-shanghai/

Gidleigh Park Hotel

The Gidleigh Park Hotel is a luxury hotel and restaurant located in Gidleigh, near Chagford, Devon, England. This charming hotel is positioned on the banks of the river Teign, and enjoys an exceptional location right on the edge of Dartmoor National Park. This context helps to create an atmosphere of tranquility and romance within a Tudor-style country house, beautifully furnished by the Brownsword family.

https://www.itinerariesperienziali.it/en/directory-offerte/listing/gidleigh-park-hotel/

2. The Principles of the Experiential Path in practice

We will now delve deeper into the ten principles of the Experiential Path, clarifying them with operational examples and real case studies.

2.1. Multisensoriality

Principle 1: Multisensorial

The experiential path must include multisensory activities (involvement of the senses: **sight, hearing, touch, smell** and, where possible, **taste**).

A multisensory experiential journey sees the involvement of multiple senses, even without direct participation of the guests, in the activities that constitute the experience.

For example, when tasting typical products, at least the following senses are stimulated: sight, taste, smell and hearing.

Direct experiences and observations made on the field involve the involvement of most of the senses: sight, hearing, touch, smell and, in some cases, taste.

Contact with nature, animals and food offer countless opportunities for multisensory experiences.

A walk in the fields or production sites in a rural environment can be the occasion for a truly unique multisensory experience: perceiving the effects of the wind on the skin, the sound of insects or animals, the smell of flowers, hay, crushed grapes, wine, pressed oil, aromatic herbs, as well as touching with your hands flowers, animals, trees and everything that we come across during the walk (apart from the nettles, I wouldn't recommend going that far!)

Some events often integrated with the experiential offer, such as excursions and guided tours, are in themselves multisensory events. In this case, the first principle is to be considered endogenous; in other cases, such as services for people, entertainment, or the very arrangement of the rooms and common areas of the structure in which one is a guest, of the tables and of the food itself, it is often a question of adding elements that enrich the experience: **shine, herbs, sounds, immersive environments** and other sensory stimuli. In the case of Guest Experiences, the habit of using environmental aromas wisely is widespread; in the Wellness Experiences also that of integrating the journey with tasting of herbal teas and/or tastings of wines or typical products (obviously in harmony with the context of the experience and the creation of a stimulating and particularly relaxing visual environment).

Help is therefore given by using techniques and methodologies typical of **Sensory Marketing**.

Perfumes, in addition to enhancing and improving taste, as is the case with food and wine offerings, can also be used to stimulate positive memories and mental associations.

In some cases, background aromas are used (**atmospheric aromas**) to create a particular atmosphere or climate that serves to strengthen the experience (whether linked to the food and wine service, or linked to other types of services, such as a stay in an accommodation facility, or in a wellness centre, or staying inside a store).

Charles Spence, in his book "Gastrophysics: the new science of eating", tells how his grandfather, who had a grocery shop in the north of England, scattered first-class coffee beans on the floor, in the space behind the counter. When a customer entered, he would crush the beans with his foot, releasing an aroma into the air that, he hoped, would prompt them to buy some coffee.

I have already described the multisensory experiences of the Ultraviolet Restaurant; let's see other examples:

The **Fat Duck** offers typical dishes like quail jelly and a scampi cream with liver pâté on top. The dish is served with an oak centerpiece, and the steam is released when the water is poured onto the dry ice placed on top of the moss.

https://youtu.be/8HEa68YgKJ0?si=PSWnZPEMTsyUun5_

Another example of sensorial marketing comes from the same Fat Duck restaurant, where customers, while savoring a seafood appetizer, can immerse themselves further in the experience thanks to the use of headphones that reproduce the sound of the sea.

The Fat Duck Sound of the Sea

https://youtu.be/R_6vJ4jB0B0

At **Alinea** restaurant in Chicago, *turbot with shellfish, water chestnuts and hyacinth steam* is served by pouring boiling water over a vessel that contains holes.

The choice of perfumes is also important: a choice based exclusively on one's personal tastes could lead to identifying the wrong perfume, perhaps outside the context of the product/service one wants to offer to customers, and therefore create unwanted effects.

Dunkin Donuts some time ago launched an advertising campaign to promote their coffee as a drink. The idea was to put the ad on buses in South Korea spreading the smell of coffee. To do this, they created a machine that activated that familiar scent during the ad. This way people were able to associate the scent with the brand. To be even more strategic, they selected bus routes that stopped in front of Dunkin' stores Donuts.

2.2. Cultural approach (Local identities)

Principle 2: Cultural approach (Local identities)

The experiential path must allow to **deepen the knowledge** of elements of local identity.

A cultural experience is usually associated with elements of local identity: places, stories, typical products, uses, customs and traditions. In this case the principle is endogenous. These identities can be cultural, natural, historical or demo-ethno-anthropological elements. An intelligent (and competent) *story* of these identities will ensure that the conditions are created for an emotional connection between the participant and the cultural resource object of the experiential/interpretive journey. It is a connection that will make the memory of the places and of the experience itself lasting.

Aspects to take into consideration for experiential offers, respectful of this principle:

- **Cultural Tours**: organizing tours that explore local history, architecture and identities, led by local experts who can share stories and in-depth knowledge.
- **Artisan Workshops**: offering workshops that allow guests to learn and practice local arts and crafts under the guidance of local artisans.
- **Gastronomic Experiences**: creating culinary experiences that not only allow you to savor local cuisine, but also exploring the stories, techniques and traditions behind the dishes.
- **Participation in Local Events**: including opportunities for guests to participate in festivals, ceremonies and other local events that celebrate and demonstrate local culture and traditions.
- **Exploration of Local Nature**: guiding guests through significant natural landscapes, sharing stories and facts about local flora, fauna and ecosystems.

A characteristic of typical local products is that of linking the food and wine experience to recognized local identities. In Italy, among the local products that should be taken into consideration, the Italian Traditional Agri-Food Products **(PAT)** should not be forgotten: these products are included in a specific list, prepared by the Ministry of Agricultural, Food and Forestry Policies and Tourism with the collaboration of the Regions.

By *traditional products* we mean those productions and agri-food goods of a typical nature, with traditional characteristics, whose processing, conservation and seasoning methods have been consolidated over time. The requirement to be recognized as Traditional Agri-food Products (PAT) is to be «obtained with processing, conservation and maturing methods consolidated over time, homogeneous throughout the area concerned, according to traditional rules, for a period of no less than twenty-five years.»

The local identity is also identifiable not only by the menu presented, but also by the way and place in which they are presented.

What must be clear is that, even for experiences for which the principle is not endogenous, they can be easily integrated and enriched with aspects that allow deepen your knowledge of elements of local identity: all it takes is a little intelligence and quick research into the cultural context of the place where the experience takes place. For example, within Wellness Experiences, it can be useful offer typical local products or talk about local customs and lifestyles.

Old City Hall subway station – New York

In 1904, New York's first subway ride departed from City Hall station amid great civic pride. With exclusive access through the New York Transit Museum, explore the elegant chandeliers, leaded skylights, vaulted tile ceiling, and graceful curves of this decommissioned subway station.

https://www.itinerariesperienziali.it/en/directory-offerte/listing/old-city-hall-subway-station-new-york/

The Dining Pod Restaurant, Koh Kood (Thailand)

Comfortably seated in a bamboo capsule, set high in the tropical foliage of Koh Kood's ancient rainforest, guests can gaze out over the ocean and savor local produce.

https://www.itinerariesperienziali.it/en/directory-offerte/listing/ristorante-the-dining-pod-koh-kood-thailandia/

Restaurant Le Panoramic – Chamonix

Le Panoramic Brévent Restaurant is in Chamonix, France. Its characteristic is to offer a unique culinary experience with breathtaking views of the surrounding mountains.

https://www.itinerariesperienziali.it/en/directory-offerte/listing/ristorante-le-panoramic-chamonix/

Villa Escudero near the Lebasin Falls – Philippines

The experience offered by the Le Bascate Labasin restaurant consists in the possibility of enjoying the traditional Filipino lunch, kamayan style, with your feet immersed in the shallow running water, close to the Lebasin waterfalls.

https://www.itinerariesperienziali.it/en/directory-offerte/listing/ristorante-le-cascate-labasin-filippine/

2.3. Uniqueness

Principle 3: Uniqueness

The experiential path must present **unique** characteristics.

The uniqueness of the cultural experience or one centered on unusual, spectacular places, with a strong cultural connotation or of significant national or international relevance, lies precisely in its nature (endogenous principle).

An authentic cultural experience is not, in general, a serial or mass offering. The products and services possibly included in the experiential path are only an indirect aspect, the essential components are emotions, sensations, the ability to make people *feel* and *discover* something different from the usual, and therefore *unique*.

For example, a food and wine event within an ancient village presents unique characteristics linked precisely to the fact that it is linked to culturally unique paths, as each village has its own uniqueness that characterizes it. The same can be said for the cultural and natural attractions of the place.

Even when the experiences concern used (and reused) aspects, such as the Hard Rock Cafes and the various food and wine initiatives whose theme is also used frequently (see the medieval themed dinners). We could say that, since each place (and related context) can be considered unique in its nature, the principle is respected.

Aspects to take into consideration for experiential offers, respectful of this principle, are the following:

- **Exclusive Events**: creating events or experiences that are offered only in specific periods or contexts, such as a food and wine event in an ancient village.
- **Exclusive Access**: offering access to places or experiences that are otherwise inaccessible to the public, such as a private visit to a historical or cultural site.
- **Personalized Experiences**: creating experiences that are personalized for guests, considering their interests and preferences.

- **Unique Stories**: sharing local stories and legends that are unique to the location, enriching the experience with special narratives and anecdotes.
- **Local interaction**: facilitating authentic interactions with the local community, allowing guests to truly immerse themselves in the local culture.

Tramjazz – Rome

Tramjazz is an evening of entertainment that offers a jazz concert, an excellent candlelit dinner and a night tour in the center of Rome, all aboard a historic tram from the ATAC collection, restored and rearranged as a restaurant and concert hall traveling.

https://www.itinerariesperienziali.it/en/directory-offerte/listing/tramjazz-roma/

Dinner in the sky

These experiences work through to a platform suspended from the ground by a 50-meter-high crane, and take place from time to time in different places.

https://www.itinerariesperienziali.it/en/directory-offerte/listing/dinner-in-the-sky/

Ali Barbour's Cave Restaurant – Kenya

At Dani Beach, thirty kilometers south of Mombasa, a long staircase leads to a restaurant housed inside a natural coral quarry located ten meters below sea level, and illuminated by hundreds of candles that create a particular play of chiaroscuro.

https://www.itinerariesperienziali.it/en/directory-offerte/listing/ali-barbours-cave-restaurant-kenia/

Ithaa Undersea Restaurant – Maldives

Dine five meters below the ocean surface in the underwater restaurant, with panoramic views of the coral gardens and fusion menus paired with fine wines.

https://www.itinerariesperienziali.it/en/directory-offerte/listing/ithaa-undersea-restaurant-maldive/

Giraffe Manor Hotel

The Giraffe Manor Hotel in Nairobi, Kenya offers an extraordinary and unparalleled experience. Here, guests not only enjoy a luxurious stay, they can also interact in an intimate and unique way with nature and wildlife. In the Giraffe Manor it is possible to come into direct contact with giraffes, providing an authentic and memorable experience.

One of the most fascinating features of this hotel is the presence of the resident herd of Rothschild giraffes. These magnificent creatures regularly visit the facility, poking their long necks through the windows, hoping for a treat, before retreating to their forest sanctuary.

https://www.itinerariesperienziali.it/en/directory-offerte/listing/giraffe-manor-hotel/

Principle 4: Relational approach (centrality and uniqueness of people)

The experiential path must be based on **human relationships**.

To apply this principle, it is important to consider the aspects that are valid for any experience, use empathetic communication and personalize the experience based on the guest's personality and expectations.

An experience must be characterized by a strong human relationship that is created between those who offer the experience and those who receive it.

The capacity for empathic communication that those who offer the experience should have (in particular, the staff who encounter the guests) and receiving *sensations*, are factors linked to the relationships that are created during the experience, an aspect that it happens easily in the presence of a limited number of people who take advantage of the experiential offer at the same time. A real and authentic experience is hardly an offer aimed at a mass of people.

Aspects to take into consideration for experiential offers, respectful of this principle:

- **Attentive staff**: making sure staff are trained and skilled in communicating and interacting with guests in an empathetic and attentive manner.
- **Small Group Experiences**: offering small group experiences to maintain authenticity and enable a deeper connection between guests and staff.
- **Authentic Interactions**: creating opportunities for authentic interactions with the local community, such as shared meals, workshops or community events.
- **Active Listening**: paying attention to guests' needs, interests and feedback, tailoring the experience accordingly.
- **Personal Stories**: sharing personal stories and local experiences, allowing guests to see and understand the culture and place from an insider's perspective.

Principle 5: Direct participation

The experiential path must include the **direct participation** of the guest in some activities. Direct participation is one of the elements underlying the concept of *immersion*. Direct participation makes the users of the experience become aware actors who are not, therefore, passive spectators of the event.

In some cases, the very typology of the offer, as enjoyed in immersive places or for example, in strong contact with nature, is such that this principle is to be considered endogenous. Same consideration where services are provided which involve the direct participation of guests (excursions, sports activities, wellness activities, experiences carried out in production centers, interactive safaris where, in addition to observing wildlife, guests can participate in animal tracking, etc.).

In all other types of experiences, it is necessary, if you want to apply the principle of direct participation, to create moments that see the direct involvement of the guests, perhaps using technology and making guests interact with the surrounding environment, or creating moments of entertainment that involves the involvement of those present.

Here are some examples:

- **Craft workshops** where guests can learn ancient crafts, such as weaving, ceramics or woodworking, creating their own artefacts.
- **Artistic workshops** in which it is possible to acquire knowledge, through participation, on aspects such as painting, sculpture, photography and writing.
- **Cultural and traditional experiences** in which guests themselves can be part of traditional festivities and ceremonies, learning and participating in rituals.
- **Agricultural activities** where guests can participate in the daily activities of a farm, such as milking, harvesting or planting.

An example: *u pani cunzatu.*

Let's consider the case of the experiential offer of *seasoned bread* (*cunzatu* bread) made according to ancient peasant traditions, typical of Southern Italy, in particular of Sicily. We hypothesize that the offer allows you to experience some salient moments of the bread-making process: kneading, leavening, shaping and baking, to which are added the phase of *cunzatura*, and that of tasting the freshly baked bread and *cunzatu*; all in the name of conviviality experienced with the baker and the housewives who organized the offer.

Let's assume that in some phases the direct intervention of the participants is expected (e.g. mixing, shaping, cooking, etc.) and that the offer also includes a short activity that illustrates how the various phases of bread making were carried out, according to tradition. , and show the work tools, the choice of wood, the techniques for controlling the oven and cleaning the bread at the end of cooking.

We also assume that the offer is presented taking care of some aesthetic aspects (environment and instruments that recall ancient periods, characters dressed in a traditional way) and finally, that there is the presence of some short moments of entertainment, in harmony and contextualized with the theme characterizing the offering (the preparation of bread in ancient traditions).

In the case just mentioned, all the elements that characterize an experiential offer in the full sense exist. In this case we can say that the participant *puts his hands in the dough*, and all five senses are involved: sight, hearing, touch, smell and taste. Furthermore, you learn something about ancient local traditions through immersion in an event that will be unforgettable.

If, however, some elements characterizing the experience are missing, such as the direct involvement of the participants, and the offer is limited, for example, to the simple tasting of freshly baked bread, we are not in the presence of a cultural experiential offer in the full sense.

Tasting activities should not be limited to just tasting, but to moments of direct interactions, aimed at stimulating the curiosity of those present, asking guests to prepare something themselves (even a few moments are enough), recognize the aromas or the different angles that can offer similar foods and drinks (cheeses, wines, liqueurs, etc.)

Sometimes we see food and wine offers called "experiential" which are limited to the simple tasting of typical local products, in which the learning component through direct participation and links with the elements of identity and uniqueness of the territory is missing. In these cases, we can legitimately talk about an offer linked to food and wine tourism, which is always a form of stimulating cultural tourism and of a certain interest, but not an offer linked to experiential tourism.

Hard Rock Cafe - Aya Napa

The Hard Rock Cafe -Aya Napa (Cyprus) features large interactive screens where guests can select famous objects related to the rock world (guitars and other instruments), magnify them to obtain information, or activate sounds.

https://www.itinerariesperienziali.it/en/directory-offerte/listing/hard-rock-cafe-aya-napa/

Principle 6: Experiential learning

The experiential path must include a learning phase through the direct participation of the guest in some activities.

Educational, food and wine and cultural experiences, especially if achieved through direct participation, are forms of learning: in fact, they allow you to learn something new through the learning model called *Experiential Learning*, which sees direct involvement and physical in the activities associated with the tourist offer (e.g. cooking, harvesting, milking, making artisanal products, etc.) and through the involvement, if possible, of the 5 senses: sight, hearing, taste, smell and above all, touch. The 5 senses are certainly involved in experiential offers related to food and wine. In others, such as the creation of artisanal products, taste may not be stimulated, but it certainly remains a multisensory experience if all the other senses are activated and if there is real and direct participation.

A similar argument is valid for an excursion, especially if it is not limited to a simple walk in nature and is accompanied by a description of the places, local flora and fauna, stories, local traditions or knowledge of local identities. An aspect not to be overlooked is to include, within the naturalistic excursion, experiential training moments such as the collection of spontaneous vegetables (mustard, chicory, wild fennel, etc.) accompanied by the explanation that allows you to recognize them and other aspects which describe how they can be linked to local, possibly gastronomic, traditions.

Many of the examples presented for principle 5 (direct participation) can in fact also be taken as reference for the principle just described.

Aspects to take into consideration for experiential offers, respectful of this principle:

- **Workshops and hands-on activities**: offering workshops and hands-on activities, such as cooking, making crafts or participating in collections, that allow guests to learn by doing.

- **Educational excursions**: organizing excursions that not only explore natural beauty, but also educate guests about local flora, fauna, geology and culture.
- **Guided tastings**: offering tastings of local foods and drinks that not only satisfy the palate, but also educate guests about local production processes, traditions and stories.
- **Cultural Interactions**: creating opportunities for guests to learn through interaction with the local community, participating in traditions, ceremonies and other cultural activities.

The Culinary Institute of America (CIA) – USA

The Culinary Institute of America offers cooking classes and workshops for both cooking enthusiasts and professionals, allowing them to *learn by doing*. Participants not only learn culinary techniques, but also actively immerse themselves in the preparation of dishes, directly experimenting with ingredients and techniques.

Link to the institute: https://www.ciachef.edu

Link to the presentation video: https://youtu.be/cQ7C4diTAFU

Shark Cage Diving – South Africa

Great White Shark Cage Diving: in addition to the thrilling experience, operators often provide in-depth information about sharks and their behaviors, contributing to hands-on, hands-on learning about marine conservation.

https://www.sharkcagediving.net/

Link to a presentation video:

https://youtu.be/aFzsiqMxy0A?si=pCgEwHpkiqtRiXX6

Traditional Japanese Tea Ceremony – Japan

It entails the participation in a traditional Japanese tea ceremony. Visitors not only observe, but also actively participate, learning skills and traditions through direct practice.

https://tea-ceremony-kyoto.com/

Video: https://youtu.be/ECZSY9iiSi4?si=nblJlxzz6pmO9vfb

The Irish Whiskey Experience – Ireland

A center dedicated to learning the art of whiskey tasting and its production. In addition to guided tastings, visitors can take part in courses to create their own whiskey blend, learning through first-hand experience.

https://www.irishwhiskeyexperience.net/

Cook and taste

This is an initiative proposed by a Trentino restaurant, where it is possible to access the kitchen to prepare, and subsequently taste, local recipes together with the chef.

https://www.itinerariesperienziali.it/en/directory-offerte/listing/cucina-e-gusta/

Principle 7: Thematic approach

Each experiential path must be built starting from a **theme** that characterizes it and which constitutes its common thread. The theme represents the starting point of the experience: it is in fact the common thread that allows you to identify the place, the plot and the most suitable scenography elements to make the experience real. The theme is the first attractive element that must be communicated to potential users of the experience path. È extremely important, especially for cultural experiential itineraries, that the theme is chosen in harmony with the identified places and the territory to which they belong.

The thematic approach is widely used in the field of experiences, it is no coincidence that it is one of the main elements of staging experiences (theatre as a model of experience).

Some examples of practical application of this principle are the following:

1. Thematic food and wine tours

- **Theme**: the traditional cuisine of a specific region.
- **Application**: organizing tours that explore local food and drink production, with tastings, cooking demonstrations and meetings with local producers, all focusing on regional specialties.

2. Historical-Cultural Trips

- **Theme**: the medieval era in an ancient city.
- **Application**: creating experiences that include costumed guided tours, medieval events and fairs, as well as interactive activities (such as falconry or sculpture workshops) that immerse visitors in medieval times.

3. Offers related to the Wellness Experience

- **Theme**: connection with nature for mental and physical well-being.
- **Application**: offering activities, such as sunrise yoga in nature, guided hikes focused on mindfulness, and workshops on local medicinal herbs, all designed to reconnect participants with the natural environment.

4. Ecological Adventures

- **Theme**: the conservation of marine life.
- **Application**: organizing guided dives, workshops on marine conservation and volunteer beach clean-ups, while providing information and training on protecting marine ecosystems.

5. Festivals and Artistic Events

- **Theme**: contemporary art in a particular movement or style.
- **Application**: creating a festival that celebrates contemporary art through exhibitions, workshops with artists, and guided tours of galleries and studios, with a focus on a specific artistic movement.

6. Urban Explorations

- **Theme**: the modernist architecture of a city.
- **Application**: offering walking or cycling tours that explore modernist buildings and structures, with discussions and lectures on the evolution of modernist architecture and its impact on the city.

7. Educational Camps for Children

- **Theme**: the discovery of local wildlife.
- **Application**: creating summer or weekend camps for children that include activities such as animal tracking, wildlife viewing, and creating animal shelters, all with an educational focus on local wildlife.

8. Artisan Workshops

- **Theme**: the art of traditional ceramics.
- **Application**: organizing workshops that not only teach ceramic techniques, but also its history and cultural significance in the region, with visits to local workshops and ceramic museums.

Here are some real examples:

Gardaland Adventure Hotel

Gardaland Adventure Hotel is a structure that has 100 rooms all themed according to 4 settings: *Arctic, Arabian, Jungle* and *Wild West*, distributed between two pavilions immersed in a completely themed context.

https://youtu.be/9O5GPWqmiGQ?si=LeLtvZaUtqfeOBYH

Barbie Café, Taipei (Taiwan)

Themed restaurant, licensed by Mattel, the Barbie manufacturer; it attracts attention for its design and atmosphere, completely immersed in the world of Barbie. The restaurant also features a giant Barbie box that allows customers to feel like a life-size Barbie. The maids wear tutus and tiaras, while their male colleagues try to look like Ken, Barbie's boyfriend.

https://www.itinerariesperienziali.it/en/directory-offerte/listing/barbie-cafe-taipei-taiwan/

Wilde Bar & Restaurant – Chicago

Thematic bar inspired by Oscar Wilde; on the fireplace there is a portrait of Oscar Wilde made by Andy Warhol.

https://www.itinerariesperienziali.it/en/directory-offerte/listing/wilde-bar-restaurant-chicago/

2.8. Aesthetic approach

Principle 8: Aesthetic approach

The aesthetic approach is one of the elements, together with that of direct participation, at the basis of the concept of *immersion.* The events that constitute 'the staging of the experience' must be designed in such a way as to give importance to all aspects that can influence aesthetics: the atmosphere, the sense of beauty, the place chosen for the experience, the plot (screenplay) which must be consistent with the chosen theme and the identified location.

Particular care must be taken to favor the sensory stimuli that harmonize the experience, eliminating as much as possible the negative cues that could disturb its enjoyment.

The concept of aesthetics, understood as what we perceive as beautiful through our senses, can be linked to an artfully created environment or even to contexts linked to particularly stimulating panoramas, landscapes, artefacts or cultural places.

Tilden, in relation to the experiential paths of interpretation of cultural heritage, writes that among the countless aspects of beauty, the interpreter essentially deals with the following four:

- The contact through the visitor's senses with the beauty of the panoramas and landscapes – with "wildness"; it is axiomatic that natural beauty, perceived through the senses, does not need interpretation: it interprets itself.
- The beauty of the mind's adventure: the revelation of the order of nature.
- The beauty of the product: man's aspiration to create beautiful things.
- The beauty of the conduct or behavior of which man has shown himself capable.

In some cases, it is useful to remember what Blaise Pascal wrote, quoted by Freeman Tilden:

> *Too much noise deafens us; too much light blinds us; too much distance or too closeness prevents us from seeing; a speech that is too long or too short makes it obscure; too much truth disconcerts us*[5].

or simply the old local saying: 'Too much breaks the bag'.

---

[5] **Freeman Tilden – Interpretare il nostro Patrimonio cap. 10: "Niente in eccesso".**

The following aspects must be taken into consideration for experiential offers, respectful of this principle:

- **Thoughtful Design**: paying attention to all aspects of experience design, including environments, sounds, smells, and sights.
- **Thematic Experiences**: creating experiences that follow a specific theme, ensuring that every aspect of the experience aligns with this theme.
- **Eliminate Distractions**: removing or minimizing elements that may distract or detract from the desired experience.
- **Natural and Created Beauty**: taking advantage of both the natural beauty of the environment and the aesthetic elements created to enrich the experience.
- **Balance**: mantaining balance in the use of aesthetic elements, avoiding excesses that could be overwhelming or distracting.

Sirocco Restaurant, Bangkok (Thailand)

In this case the principle linked to the aesthetic approach is a consequence of both an environment created and by its landscape; in fact, the Sirocco Sky Bar is a restaurant in Bangkok considered the *highest* open-air restaurant in the world. Located on the 63rd floor, the restaurant offers its customers breathtaking views, an emblematic and spectacular dome and food prepared by some of the most eclectic chefs in Asia. The design of the venue is inspired by Mediterranean atmospheres.

https://www.itinerariesperienziali.it/en/directory-offerte/listing/ristorante-sirocco-bangkok-thailandia/

Joel Robuchon Restaurant – Las Vegas

The environment has been artfully created to resemble a luxurious Art Deco residence, complete with a lush garden terrace and marble floors. Particular attention is paid to all the details including the playing of classical music and meticulous attention to the plating.

https://www.itinerariesperienziali.it/en/directory-offerte/listing/ristorante-joel-robuchon-las-vegas/

Kitcho Arashiyama Honten Restaurant, Kyoto

The restaurant does not use high technology, but focuses on an atmosphere that enhances the beauty of the environments created respecting Japanese culture. Each of its seven dining rooms has views of a Japanese garden, with a scenery that changes with the seasons, slightly different from day to day, helping to create a truly one-of-a-kind dining experience.

https://www.itinerariesperienziali.it/en/directory-offerte/listing/ristorante-kitcho-arashiyama-honten-kyoto/

Hotel Eremito – Holidays in the Monastery

Eremito is a mystical place, the sense of aesthetics is linked to the place; the Umbrian valleys, in which it is immersed, amplify the sense of spirituality of the hotel, but also a consequence of the care with which the entire hospitality path was designed.

https://www.itinerariesperienziali.it/en/directory-offerte/listing/hotel-eremito-vacanze-in-monastero/

The Blue Lagoon, Iceland

The Blue Lagoon is a geothermal spa that offers a unique aesthetic experience thanks to its lunar landscape and turquoise waters in a black lava context.

https://www.bluelagoon.com/

Keukenhof Gardens, Holland

Keukenhof is one of the largest gardens in the world, offering a stunning visual experience when millions of bulbs bloom in spring.

https://keukenhof.nl/en/

Cherry Blossom Viewing, Japan

Watching cherry blossoms (*sakura*) in Japan is an aesthetic and cultural experience, where natural beauty becomes the epicenter of the experience.

https://www.japan-guide.com/sakura/

2.9. Entertainment

Principle 9: Entertainment

The experiential path should also include **moments of entertainment** that enrich and make the experience pleasant. At the same time, they 'lighten' the user's experience, making the entire journey pleasant with moments of pure absorption. We must not forget that the users of an experiential offer choose the experience above all to satisfy their desire for pleasure.

Aspects to take into consideration for experiential offers, respectful of this principle:

- **Fun Activities**: integrating activities that are purely for fun, such as games, contests, or playtime.
- **Shows**: offering shows or performances, such as live music, dancing, or theater, that can enrich the experience.
- **Relaxing moments**: providing opportunities for relaxation and leisure, allowing guests to absorb and enjoy the environment at their leisure.
- **Light Interactions**: creating moments of interaction that are light and playful, allowing guests to connect with each other in a friendly and non-demanding way.
- **Pleasant Surprises**: introducing surprise or unexpected elements that can delight and amaze guests.

Cabaret Restauranty Show, Bogota – Santa Bárbara

Located in Bogota in the Santa Bárbara neighborhood, this restaurant offers shows and entertainment that, reflecting local culture and traditions, can be considered unique.

https://www.itinerariesperienziali.it/en/directory-offerte/listing/cabaret-restauranty-show-bogota-santa-barbara/

Maison Restaurant – Milan

The Maison in Milan offers a dining experience combined with entertainment shows. It creates a show every evening, offering a variety of entertainment such as burlesque, circus, live music and other types of entertainment.

https://www.itinerariesperienziali.it/en/directory-offerte/listing/ristorante-maison-milano/

Twisted Circus – performance at the Cafe de Paris

The Café de Paris is a nightclub in London located on Coventry Street, in the West End. It often hosts the Twisted Circus show, consisting of aerial acrobatics, fire games, stilt walking and other forms of entertainment.

https://www.itinerariesperienziali.it/en/directory-offerte/listing/twisted-circus-esibizione-al-cafe-de-paris/

2.10. Immersion

Principle 10: Immersion

The principle of immersion is the direct consequence of the application of the principles of multisensory, direct participation and aesthetic approach. Immersive techniques can be implemented to create a scenic environment that sees participants immersed in a multisensory context.

Look at the following image related to the Pine and Gilmore model (we have analyzed it already in the first chapter) The second dimension (along the vertical axis) describes the type of connection or environmental relationship that unites the participants with the event or performance, represented. It starts from *absorption*, where the experience 'penetrates' into the person through the mind (e.g. when watching a film on TV) up to *immersion*, where the person 'enters' the experience physically or virtually taking part in the experience itself.

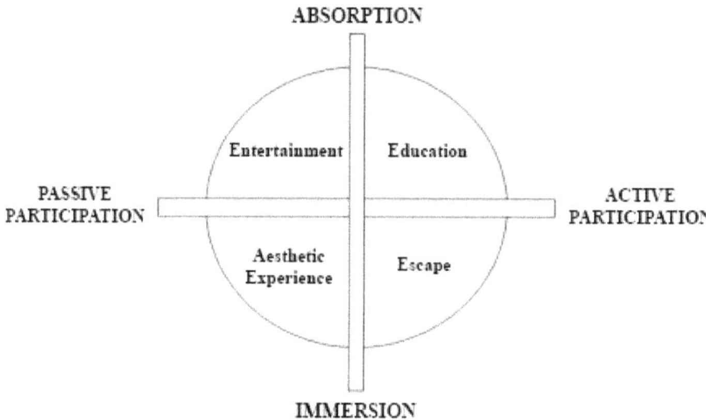

As with the aesthetic approach, some experiential paths are immersive by their very nature. This is the case of experiences that see visitors in direct contact with nature, or other aspects of cultural heritage. In this case the principle is applied for the simple fact that visitors are immersed in the surrounding environment, above all if they are active participants in the experience.

The design of an experiential path must therefore include immersive activities that directly involve the participant in multisensory activities and which involve him not only from a manual and tactile point of view, but also intellectually and emotionally.

The following aspects must be taken into consideration for experiential offers, respectful of this principle:

- **Thematic Environments**: creating environments that are completely aligned with the theme of the experience, ensuring that every detail contributes to the desired atmosphere.
- **Immersive Technology**: using technology, such as virtual or augmented reality, to enrich the environment and provide experiences that might not otherwise be possible.
- **Engaging Narrative**: developing a narrative that is engaging and interesting, guiding guests through the experience in a way that captures their imagination.
- **Authentic Interactions**: providing opportunities for authentic and meaningful interactions, both with people and the environment, which can enrich the immersive experience.
- **Exploration**: giving guests the freedom to explore and discover the environment and experience in their own way, allowing them to immerse themselves in the way they choose.

Immersive exhibitions at the Atelier des Lumières in Paris

In April 2018, the first Digital Arts Center in the French capital was inaugurated in Paris, in rue Saint-Maur. The Atelier des Lumières takes the place of an ancient Parisian foundry, the Chemin Vert, and offers its visitors monumental immersive exhibitions. With 120 video projectors and spatialized sound, the images are projected onto a surface of 3300 m^2 on walls more than 10 meters high.

The Atelier des Lumières welcomes visitors in two different spaces: The Halle of 1500 m^2 and The Studio of 160 m^2. In the first, a cycle of digital exhibitions with a long program, dedicated to the great painters of art history, are continuously projected and in the other, a shorter program is performed, dedicated to more contemporary figures.

https://www.itinerariesperienziali.it/en/directory-offerte/listing/mostre-immersive-allatelier-des-lumieres-di-parigi/

Vincent Van Gogh Alive

Immersive exhibition at the Atelier des Lumières in Paris.

https://youtu.be/BbgrHnbgoDU

Immersive Show Dinner – Villa Borghese – Rome

The Little House Valadier, presenting this *Immersive Show Dinner*, located in the heart of Villa Borghese, offers an experience that arises from the integration of food and wine excellence, images, music, live performances and special effects.

https://www.itinerariesperienziali.it/en/directory-offerte/listing/immersive-show-dinner-italia-villa-borghese-roma/

San Michele Museum

The museum offers a truly unique immersive experience thanks to interactive multimedia tools and content, capable of transmitting information and, above all, emotions regarding the events of the Italian-Austrian front, which affected Mount San Michele and the Lower Isonzo front. The Museum allows you to experience firsthand the events of the Great War on Mount San Michele: a unique and engaging journey through interactive 2D maps and 3D reconstructions of the Cima 3 gun tunnel and the cave named after General Lukachich.

https://www.itinerariesperienziali.it/en/directory-offerte/listing/museo-del-san-michele/

Feuerstein Nature Family Resort

The Feuerstein Nature Family Resort is a hotel that offers a unique and immersive experience for families seeking a vacation, and combines luxury, nature and adventure activities.

The hotel is surrounded by nature, offering an authentic and one-of-a-kind experience, where families can connect with their surroundings and enjoy the beauty and tranquility of the surrounding mountains and forests.

The activities offered are designed to allow guests to explore and interact with the natural environment, thanks also to different possibilities that include excursions, explorations and other outdoor activities that allows the user to experience nature in a direct, personal and, above all, immersive.

https://www.itinerariesperienziali.it/en/directory-offerte/listing/feuerstein-nature-family-resort/

3. Repertoire of experiential activities

Once the definitions that clarify the meaning of experiential tourism have been provided, and the principles that underlie the concept of experience itself have been identified, it can certainly be useful to identify the types of activities to which it is possible to apply these principles, which constitute the scope of application of the experiential offerings.

At this point, the 'Repertoire of Experiential Activities', as I call it, takes shape. This repertoire can be considered as a classification of experiential activities. Since the study is in its infancy, and in the future it may be possible to add further categories or subcategories, or even evaluate whether to move some activities from one category to another, I have hypothesized assigning a revision number to the repertoire that will take into account the evolution of the given classification over time.

Repertoire of Experiential Activities (Rev. 1.2):

- **Dinner Experience (DIE)**:
    - Show Cooking Experience
    - Sensorial Dinner Experience
    - Location Dinner Experience
    - Narrative Dinner Experience
    - Dinner Show Experience
    - Art Dinner Experience
    - School Dinner Experience
- **Guest Experience (GUE):**
    - Sensorial Guest Experience
    - Narrative Guest Experiences
    - Location Guest Experience, which also includes the following types:
        - *Seaside Village Experience*
        - *Farmhouse Experience*
        - *Glamping Experience*
    - Integrative Guest Experiences

- **Cultural Heritage Experience (CHE):**
  - Food and Wine Experience
  - Heritage Sides Experience
  - Intangible Cultural Heritage Experience, which includes the following typology:
    - *Hand-made Experience*
  - Cultural Expositive Experience, which also includes the following types:
    - *Museum/Ecomuseum Experience*
    - *Immersive Art Experience*
  - Cultural Entertainment Experience
  - Cultural Learning Experience
  - Heritage Interpretation Experience
- **Open-Air Experience (OAE):**
  - Trekking and Hiking Experience
  - Bike Experience
  - Diving Experience
  - Speleology Experience
  - River Experience
  - Horse Experience
  - Donkey Experience
  - Animal Experience
  - Marine Life Experience
  - Flight Experience
  - Fishing Tourism Experience
- **Wellness Experience (WLE)**
- **Entertainment and Show Experience (ESE)**
- **Sports Experience (SPE)**
- **Experiential Marketing (EMA)**

The classification of experiential activities should not be seen in a strict sense, as a type of experience can fit into more than one category. For example, Glamping Experiences and, in some cases, Farmhouse Experiences are also considered Open-Air Experiences which, in the repertoire of experiential activities 1.2, for practical reasons and to highlight the aspect linked to hospitality, have been included within the Guest Experience category. The same goes for Sport Experiences, especially for those sports in direct contact with nature, for which I have provided their own category, but which can also be classified as OAE.

However, the Open-Air Experience has close contacts with many other open field experiences included in other categories (Dinner Experiences in trees or amid nature, Cultural Heritage Experiences and Wellness Experiences in naturalistic sites, etc.).

In many cases, the relationship between the different types of experiences is very close, as in the case of Seaside Village Experiences (Fishing Tourism), Dinner Experiences, Guest Experiences and Open-Air Experiences (Fishing Tourism). The placement in one or the other category was also a choice of convenience, trying to consider, in the presence of multiple approaches, the prevailing one.

The updated version of the repertoire can be consulted at the following web address:

https://www.itinerariesperienziali.it/en/repertorio-delle-attivita-esperienziali/

3.1 Dinner Experience (DIE)

The atmosphere and multi-sensorial nature are some of the essential elements for offering what are called experiential meals. As a rule, such meals can be based on various approaches, in which we focus on some elements characterizing the experience.

Here is a non-exhaustive list of approaches (types of food and wine experiences):

- **Demonstrative (Show Cooking):** The experience focuses on the presentation, which can be spectacular or theatrical, of the dishes or some phases related to the preparation of the dishes. (E.g. theatrical presentation).
- **Sensory (Sensorial Dinner):** The experience, thanks to a careful and accurate design of the atmosphere, is particularly focused on the stimulation of some senses (hearing, touch, sight, taste, smell).
- **Location (Location Dinner):** The experience is particularly focused on unusual, spectacular places, with a strong cultural connotation or of significant national or international importance.
- **Narrative (Narrative Dinner):** The experience is characterized by a well-defined theme and is centered on a narrative through aspects such as: culture and traditions, knowledge and ancient crafts, myths and legends, natural aspects characterizing the territory, aspects linked to places of memory (events historical, literary, film, etc.).
- **Entertainment (Dinner Show):** The experience focuses on events of a predominantly entertainment nature (theatrical show, musical show, games and magic shows, etc.)
- **Exhibition (Art Dinner):** The experience focuses on exhibition events (painting, photography, contemporary art, etc.).
- **Training (School Dinner):** The experience is associated with a cooking class and generally linked to typical products.

The different approaches are not necessarily distinct, as they are often present at the same time. For example, an experiential lunch linked to a certain historical event could use different approaches simultaneously: narrative, entertainment, exhibition and sensorial, and could take place in the same location where the historical event that inspired the experience you want took place propose. In the case of the presence of multiple approaches, it may be useful, for the purpose of an initial classification, to identify the prevailing approach.

As in other types of experiences, the different approaches can be seen from different points of view. For example, the narrative, entertainment, exhibition and educational approaches can be considered as aspects that strengthen the food and wine experience, understood as a central element of reference, or the opposite can happen: the food and wine experience serves to enrich the event (narrative, cultural, educational).

Show Cooking

The experience focuses on the presentation, either spectacular or theatrical, of the dishes or some phases related to their preparation:

«Restaurants are like stages; waiters and chefs in some of the best venues in the world are increasingly playing the part of actors and magicians. Before there was only the atmosphere, today we talk about theatre, storytelling and magic at mealtimes: this is the heart, the deep soul, of the *off-the-plate* food experience. » (Charles Spence – Gastrophysics – The new science of eating).

An example of a theatrical plating method that involves a live performance is that of the Alinea restaurant in Chicago, in which the desserts are plated directly on the diners' table (show cooking).

Some examples:

Final Dessert of 20 Course Meal at Alinea

https://youtu.be/qofsdSMuGbg

5 Super Fruits Watermelon Decoration Ideas

https://youtu.be/XroJApLyApI

25 Easy Plating Techniques – Plate like a Pro

https://youtu.be/c01s-UVxoQk

Types of Colorful Plating techniques

https://www.youtube.com/watch?v=kn5DT_NvXyw

Again, for demonstration purposes, the habit of having diners visit the kitchen to see the chefs at work is spreading. This practice also goes by the name of show cooking.

Show cooking can have a demonstration or educational purpose (cooking class):

Teppanyaki

Here is an example in which the chef spectacularly prepares an *omelette* on the griddle, involving the spectators by throwing pieces of omelette onto the plates and directly to the diners so that they can catch them.

https://www.youtube.com/watch?v=r3UEiq_KGzU

Show cooking

Another example of dishes made in front of the customer.

https://youtu.be/06hdRhxJBH8

Sensorial Dinner

The experience, thanks to careful and accurate planning of the atmosphere, is particularly focused on the stimulation of multiple senses (hearing, touch, sight, taste, smell). This aspect has already been addressed in the previous chapters, where the influence of the senses on flavors was discussed.

Sublimotion Experience

Sublimotion is a restaurant located in Sant Josep de sa Talaia, Ibiza, Spain, run by two-Michelin-star chef Paco Roncero. In the restaurant there is a single table which, on two evening shifts, seats 12 people at a time. The cost of the dinner, consisting of around 20 courses, is around 1500 euros; with 18.000 euros, however, you can have the room exclusively for you and your friends. Additionally, there are 25 staff, which include expert craftsmen, chefs, illusionists, waiters and a DJ. The experience lasts about three hours in total.

https://www.itinerariesperienziali.it/en/directory-offerte/listing/ristorante-sublimotion-ibiza/

Location Dinner

The experience is particularly focused on unusual, spectacular places, with a strong cultural connotation or of significant national or international importance.

Ithaa Undersea Restaurant – Maldives

The restaurant Ithaa Undersea Restaurant in the Maldives is a one-of-a-kind dining experience, offering a 180-degree underwater view while you eat. Located 5 meters below sea level at Conrad Maldives Rangali Island in the Maldives, Ithaa offers a dining experience in an environment completely immersed in the underwater world. The name "Ithaa" means "pearl" in the local Dhivehi language. As one of the first underwater restaurants in the world, the location itself becomes an experience, immersed as it is in the crystal-clear waters of the Maldives. The view of the coral reef and marine life during your meal creates a unique multisensory experience.

https://www.itinerariesperienziali.it/en/directory-offerte/listing/ithaa-undersea-restaurant-maldive/

Dinner in the sky

Dinner in the sky is a unique concept that literally elevates the dining experience, transforming it into an extraordinary event that takes guests and gourmet cuisine into the air. This experience was first launched in Belgium and has since spread to cities around the world, offering breathtaking panoramic views while enjoying a meal prepared by renowned chefs. Guests are lifted by a crane to around 50 meters in the air, where they enjoy a meal while suspended in the air. The elevated position offers unique and spectacular views of the place below.

https://www.itinerariesperienziali.it/en/directory-offerte/listing/dinner-in-the-sky/

Chillout Ice Lounge, Dubai

The experience features ice sculptures, seating arrangements and illuminated interiors, all at a temperature of minus six degrees. Everything is frozen, including tables and chairs.

https://www.itinerariesperienziali.it/en/directory-offerte/listing/chillout-ice-lounge-dubai/

Fangweng Restaurant – Yangtze River – China

Located in Hubei Province, China, near the Sanyou Cave, or 'The Cave of the Three Travelers', Fangweng Restaurant offers a unique dining experience, being positioned along the side of a mountain, thus offering spectacular views of the Yangtze River. The restaurant is partially located in a natural cave and partially suspended along the mountainside, showing breathtaking views of the surrounding landscape.

https://www.itinerariesperienziali.it/en/directory-offerte/listing/hanging-restaurant-fangweng-in-yichang-china/

Restaurant – La Sponda – Positano

This restaurant is located in Positano, inside the *Le Sirenuse* hotel.

Positano is known for its beauty and the restaurant, located in a privileged position, allows guests to completely immerse themselves in the unique atmosphere of the place.

https://www.itinerariesperienziali.it/en/directory-offerte/listing/ristorante-la-sponda-positano/

Narrative Dinner

The food-and-wine experience is characterized by a well-defined theme and is centered on a narrative through aspects such as: culture and traditions, knowledge and ancient crafts, myths and legends, natural aspects characterizing the territory, aspects linked to places of memory (events historical, literary, film, etc.).

Sir Lancelot Restaurant – Budapest

Sir Lancelot Restaurant in Budapest is known for offering a thematic dining experience inspired by the theme of medieval knights and the round table. The restaurant's ambience recreates the atmosphere of a medieval castle, complete with period furnishings, armor and staff dressed in medieval costumes. The experience is often accompanied by live entertainment, which may include knight battles, dancing and music.

https://www.itinerariesperienziali.it/en/directory-offerte/listing/ristorante-sir-lancelot-budapest/

Club Verne, Budapest

Inspired by the book "Twenty Thousand Leagues Under the Sea".

https://www.itinerariesperienziali.it/en/directory-offerte/listing/club-verne-budapest/

Movie Restaurant – Rome

The restaurant is a real museum dedicated to cinema, with displays of movie statues, life-size replicas, Japanese robots, knights of the zodiac and much more. Each visit can offer something different thanks to the rotation of the works on display. The dishes offered take inspiration from the world of cinema and TV series, with names and presentations inspired by famous films and beloved characters. For example, dishes might have names inspired by "The Lord of the Rings," "Star Wars" or "Peppa Pig." Desserts are one of the restaurant's specialties, offering not only a pleasure for the palate but also a feast for the eyes. They are inspired by films and TV series and presented in fun and creative ways.

The experience offered by the Movie Restaurant can be associated with different subcategories of the *Dinner Experience (DIE)*:

- **Narrative Dinner:** Thanks to the strongly thematic setting and themed evenings, the restaurant creates a narrative that is intertwined with the culinary experience.
- **Location Dinner:** The unique and immersive environment of the restaurant, which serves as a cinema museum, offers a dining experience in a decidedly out of the ordinary location.
- **Entertainment (Dinner Show):** Themed evenings and special events offer entertainment and shows during dinner.

https://www.itinerariesperienziali.it/en/directory-offerte/listing/movie-restaurant-roma/

Alice of Magic World restaurant, Tokyo

The **Alice of Magic World** restaurant in Tokyo, Japan, offers a themed experience linked to the famous novel "Alice in Wonderland", by Lewis Carroll. The interiors of the restaurant are divided into different areas which include spaces dedicated to the Queen of Hearts, a garden-labyrinth with small Disney-style lounges, walls adorned with large mirrors that recall Carroll's original fairy tale and an area with giant books and a wrought iron door that evokes the atmosphere of Tim Burton.

https://www.itinerariesperienziali.it/en/directory-offerte/listing/ristorante-alice-of-magic-world-tokyo/

Dinner Show

The experience is centered on predominantly entertainment events (theatrical and musical shows, games and magic shows, etc.). Not to be confused with the theatrical approach to presenting dishes which refers to theatrical plating, or the theatrical presentation of certain stages of meal preparation.

"Il Teatro del Monastero di Cherasco" restaurant

The restaurant "Il Teatro del Monastero di Cherasco" offers a food and wine experience inside an 1700s theatre, from which it takes its name. Dinners are often accompanied by moments of entertainment which include cabaret and theater shows.

https://www.itinerariesperienziali.it/en/directory-offerte/listing/ristorante-il-teatro-del-monastero-di-cherasco/

Other examples already studied in the chapter where the principle of "entertainment" was discussed are the following:

Cabaret Restauranty Show, Bogota – Santa Bárbara

https://www.itinerariesperienziali.it/en/directory-offerte/listing/cabaret-restauranty-show-bogota-santa-barbara/

Maison Restaurant – Milan

https://www.itinerariesperienziali.it/en/directory-offerte/listing/ristorante-maison-milano/

Twisted Circus – performance at the Cafe de Paris

https://www.itinerariesperienziali.it/en/directory-offerte/listing/twisted-circus-esibizione-al-cafe-de-paris/

Art Dinner

The experience focuses on the combination of art and food, potentially enriched by artistic exhibitions (painting, photography, contemporary art, etc.) or performances during the meal.

Gallery Restaurant – Reykjavik

The Gallery Restaurant in Reykjavik offers a culinary experience of signature cuisine, served among masterpieces of painting. The elegant dining room and fine Icelandic art collection provide the perfect stage for Chef Fridgeir Ingi Eriksson's innovative culinary creations.

https://www.itinerariesperienziali.it/en/directory-offerte/listing/gallery-restaurant-reykjavik/

Cafe Jacquemart-Andre – Paris

The café is located inside a museum, so guests can enjoy viewing amazing works of art while tasting their meals.

The environment is elegant and rich in historical architectural and artistic details; thus it offers a dining experience immersed in art and culture.

https://www.itinerariesperienziali.it/en/directory-offerte/listing/cafe-jacquemart-andre-paris/

School Dinner

Experiences that include an educational component, such as cooking courses or guided tastings. These experiences are often linked to knowledge of the typical dishes of a territory.

We have already seen several examples of *School Dinner* in the chapter describing the principle of experiential learning, here are some others:

Sur La Table – United States

Sur La Table offers a variety of cooking classes, from beginner to more advanced, which often end with a dinner that includes the dishes prepared during the lesson.

https://www.surlatable.com/cooking-classes/

Jamie Oliver Cookery School – London, United Kingdom

Jamie Oliver's Cooking School offers a range of cooking classes, from homemade pasta classes to Thai cooking classes, and guests can enjoy the dishes they have prepared at the end of the class.

https://jamieolivercookeryschool.com/

Cook'n With Class – Paris, France

It offers a variety of cooking classes where guests can learn to make everything, from French croissants to gourmet dishes, and then enjoy the fruits of their labor in a meal at the end of the class.

https://cooknwithclass.com/

Sushi Making Workshop in Japan

A workshop where participants can learn the art of making sushi with expert chefs in Japan.

https://www.japanican.com/

Thai Cooking Class in Thailand

Culinary experiences where guests can learn to prepare traditional Thai dishes.

https://www.cookly.me/it-it/

3.2. Guest Experience (GUE)

A definition of **Guest Experience** is as follows:

> *Set of experiences offered to the customer/guest during the entire life cycle of their stay.*

We can think of dividing Guest Experiences into two macro-types, not necessarily different from each other:

- **Experiences linked to the structure:** experiences directly linked to the structure and the atmosphere created within it and/or to the location, which is constituted by the environment outside the structure. One or more of the approaches that have already been analyzed in the case of **Dinner Experiences** can be applied, furthermore the following approaches integrate especially well with the Guest Experience, obviously adapted to the hospitality context:
    - **Sensory Approach** (Sensorial Guest Experience)
    - **Location-based approach** (Location Guest Experience), which also includes the following types:
        - *Seaside Village Experience*
        - *Farmhouse Experience*
        - *Glamping Experience*
    - **Narrative Approach (Narrative Guest Experience)**
- **Experiences linked to integrative experiential offers**: Experiences offered to complement hospitality.

For descriptive simplicity I will call the experiences linked to the integrative experiential offers **Integrative Guest Experiences**. For these latter experiences, I refer you to the individual chapters in which I deal with this type of experience.

As indicated in the Dinner Experience chapter, different types of approaches can coexist: the Guest Experience can simultaneously present a sensorial, narrative approach or one inserted in a particular location. Where possible, it is still useful to try to identify what could be considered the prevailing approach.

In summary:

Guest Experience (GUE): Hospitality experience.

- **Sensorial Guest Experience:** hospitality experience focused particularly on the stimulation of the senses
- **Narrative Guest Experiences:** hospitality experience characterized by a well-defined theme: culture and traditions, knowledge and ancient crafts, myths and legends, natural aspects characterizing the territory, aspects linked to places of memory (historical, literary, filmic events, etc.)
- **Location Guest Experience:** hospitality experience focused particularly on unusual, spectacular places, with a strong cultural connotation or of significant national or international importance. This subcategory also includes the following types:
    - **Seaside Village Experience:** Hospitality experience that focuses on small communities located along the coast
    - **Farmhouse Experience:** Hospitality experience in a rural environment
    - **Glamping Experience:** Experience of hospitality in an environment in close contact with nature.
- **Integrative Guest Experiences:** Experiences offered to complement hospitality.

Sensorial Guest Experience

As with the Dinner Experience, the sensorial approach aims at careful design of the atmosphere, particularly focusing on the stimulation of the senses, and often creating immersive environments thanks also to the addition of elements that enrich the experience. One of the techniques often used is to introduce background aromas (atmospheric aromas) to create, through multisensory, a particular climate that serves to stimulate memories and positive mental associations.

When designing it is useful to take into account what is indicated in the model presented at the beginning of this volume "The Theater as a model of experience". The following aspects therefore become strategic:

- **Environmental context:** Intelligent use of spaces (size, shape, placement of furniture, systems, utensils and equipment), lighting, colours, smells, sounds, immersive environments and other sensory stimuli.
- **Signage**: signs, signage panels, etc. which must be pleasant, clear and consistent with the theme and the environmental context. Use welcome signs to provide information on activities that can be carried out within the facility, additional services offered in the area, etc.
- **Staff:** themed and appropriate behaviour, clothing and language.

Positive clues (stimuli) recommended

- Appropriate and engaging colors
- Adequate environmental aromas
- Sounds and background music
- Ideal temperature and suitable for the various environments (reception, rooms, common areas, corridors and services, possible wellness center, etc.)
- Theming, possibly also working on individual areas and rooms
- Comfortable materials for real physical and tactile comfort (bedding, towels, seats, etc.)
- Staff: themed and appropriate behaviour, clothing and language.

Negative clues to watch out for

- Inadequate and excessive colors
- Unpleasant odors
- Sounds and noises unrelated to context
- Background music at a volume that is too loud or not appropriate for the context
- Extremely low or high temperatures
- Materials that hinder real physical and tactile comfort (roughness, bad odors, uncomfortable, non-functional, etc.)
- Staff: inadequate behaviour, clothing and language.

It should not be thought that only luxury hotels are responsible for adopting the sensorial and immersive approach. Even small accommodation facilities, attentive to aesthetics and using sensory stimuli, may be able to offer Sensorial Guest Experiences.

Icehotel, Jukkasjärvi, Sweden

A hotel completely made of ice and snow, offering a unique sensory experience, where guests can sleep in rooms made entirely of ice.

https://www.icehotel.com/

Kakslauttanen Arctic Resort, Finland:

Guests can stay in glass igloos, enjoying views of the Northern Lights in comfortable surroundings.

https://www.itinerariesperienziali.it/en/directory-offerte/listing/kakslauttanen-arctic-resort/

Location Guest Experience

The Location Guest Experience is characterized by places with unusual, spectacular aspects, with a strong cultural connotation or of significant national or international importance.

The two previously mentioned examples (Icehotel and Kakslauttanen Arctic Resort), in addition to being considered *Sensorial Guest Experiences*, can also be defined in all respects as *Location Guest Experiences.*

Other examples as follows:

St. Regis Resort in Bora Bora

The resort, located in one of the most beautiful destinations in the world, the tropical island of Bora Bora, with its overwater villas and views of Mount Otemanu, offers a location experience that is truly exclusive.

https://www.itinerariesperienziali.it/en/directory-offerte/listing/st-regis-resort-di-bora-bora/

Sant'Angelo Luxury Resort

The Sant'Angelo Luxury Resort is located in Matera, Italy, a city known for its historic *Sassi*, ancient houses carved into the rock. The resort's unique and historic location offers a location experience that is intrinsically linked to the culture and history of the location.

https://www.itinerariesperienziali.it/en/directory-offerte/listing/santangelo-luxury-resort/

Sandals South Coast

Sandals South Coast is a tropical beachfront resort located in Jamaica. From brand new overwater bungalows to a bar and romantic overwater chapel, Sandals South Coast brings guests closer to the aquatic element than ever before. The resort is located on a two-mile stretch of white sand beach on Jamaica's south coast and is nestled in a 500-acre nature reserve.

https://www.itinerariesperienziali.it/en/directory-offerte/listing/sandals-south-coast/

Hotel Conrad Abu Dhabi Etihad Towers

Hotel Conrad Abu Dhabi Etihad Towers is known for its luxury and unique location. Located in Abu Dhabi, United Arab Emirates, the hotel is part of the Etihad Towers complex and offers spectacular views of the city and the Arabian Gulf.

https://www.itinerariesperienziali.it/en/directory-offerte/listing/hotel-conrad-abu-dhabi-etihad-towers/

Convent of San Bartolomeo

The **Convento of San Bartolomeo** relay is a historic residence located in Piancastagnaio, and precisely on the slopes of Mount Amiata. It is said that Saint Francis of Assisi himself chose the site for the first Franciscan convent of Castrum Plani Castagnarii.

https://www.itinerariesperienziali.it/en/directory-offerte/listing/convento-san-bartolomeo/

Cocoa Island by COMO, Maldives

A luxury resort offering overwater villas in an idyllic setting with white beaches and crystal-clear waters.

https://www.comohotels.com/maldives/como-cocoa-island

El Nido Resorts, Palawan, Philippines

It offers an exclusive experience in a tropical paradise, with activities such as snorkeling and diving. The unique location of the resort, with its overwater villas and views of Mount Otemanu, offers a location experience that can be considered exclusive.

https://www.elnidoresorts.com/

Seaside Village Experience

The hospitality experience that focuses on small communities located along the coast includes what in Italy is defined as Fish Tourism and Tourism in Seaside Villages. A characteristic of this type of experience is that it is linked to tourism that enhances the unique characteristics of small coastal villages, such as local culture, traditions, gastronomy, and often also uncontaminated nature and picturesque landscapes.

The **Seaside Experience** would fall within the cultural experiences; having included this type of experience among the 'Guest Experiences' simply wants to underline how the approach that often prevails is that of hospitality.

Some practical examples are as follows:

- **Ittiturismo (Italy):** This practice, also regulated at a regulatory level in Italy, is complementary to fishing tourism and consists of offering tourist services such as hospitality in fishermen's houses and seaside villages.
- **Seaside villages:** Visit small coastal villages which often offer a unique experience of discovering traditions, history and gastronomy linked to the sea and coastal life.
- **Experiences in Fishing Villages:** In different parts of the world, there are programs and tour packages that allow visitors to stay in fishing villages, learning more about their lives, fishing techniques, and local cuisine.

Without going into the merits of the individual offers, here is a list of places that could offer examples of Seaside Village Experience:

- **Mahahual Village, Costa Maya:** quiet fishing village with pristine beaches and crystal-clear waters.
- **North Wildwood, New Jersey:** a small town in New Jersey that offers attractions such as a portion of the famous Wildwood Boardwalk and the historic Hereford Inlet Lighthouse.

- **Branscombe, Devon:** Situated along the Jurassic Coast, Branscombe is a picturesque village with thatched houses and a stream running through picnic-friendly meadows to a working watermill and then to the sea.
- **Oia, Santorini, Greece:** a village that is known for its spectacular sunsets, whitewashed houses and blue-domed churches.
- **Kalk Bay, Cape Town, South Africa:** a fishing village with antique shops, cafes, art galleries and fresh fish markets.
- **Cadaqués, Spain:** fishing village with narrow cobbled streets, natural beaches and the home of artist Salvador Dalí.
- **Tossa de Mar, Spain:** a medieval village on the Costa Brava with beautiful beaches, , a castle and cobbled streets.

Farmhouse Experience

This category includes experiences linked to hospitality in a rural environment, typical of holiday farms. It is important to consider that holiday farm experiences, allowing, when adequately organized, to immerse oneself in rural everyday life and come into direct contact with activities linked to agricultural life (such as animal care, harvesting and processing of agricultural products, etc.), could be considered typical open-air activities. Their placement within the Guest Experience aims to underline the hospitality aspect.

Los Poblanos Historic Inn & Organic Farm, New Mexico, USA

An experience offering a stay on a working farm with an emphasis on cuisine and sustainable agriculture.

https://lospoblanos.com/

Fairview Farm Log Cabins, Virginia, USA

A relaxing farm experience with cooking classes, wine tastings and panoramic views of the Tuscan countryside.

https://www.fairviewfarmholidayaccommodation.co.uk/

Fattoria Barbialla Nuova, Tuscany, Italy

A holiday farm that offers authentic experiences, including truffle hunting, nature walks and Tuscan cuisine.

https://www.barbialla.it/

Blue Hill at Stone Barns, New York, USA

A holiday farm experience offering a high-quality restaurant and the opportunity to explore the working farm.

https://www.bluehillfarm.com/

Holiday Farm Fattoria Lavacchio, Tuscany, Italy

A farm experience with activities such as grape harvest, cooking classes and wine tastings.

https://guardastelle.com/

Glamping Experience

Hospitality takes place in environments in close contact with nature (tents, tree houses, transparent structures, towers and other accommodation located in direct contact with nature). **Glamping Experiences** can be considered **Open-Air Experiences** in all respects; their placement within the **Guest Experiences**, similarly to the Farmhouse Experiences, is motivated by the desire to underline the hospitality aspect.

Airstream Europe – Spain

It offers a unique experience staying in Airstream caravans in picturesque locations in Spain.

https://www.airstreameurope.com/

Treehotel – Sweden

It offers unique and luxurious accommodation in the forests of Sweden, with structures ranging from cabins suspended in trees to floating 'UFOs'.

https://treehotel.se/en/

Whitepod – Switzerland

It consists of geodesic pods (dome tents) that offer luxury and comfort in the middle of the Swiss Alps, offering a unique and sustainable experience.

https://whitepod.com/

EcoCamp Patagonia – Chile

It offers geodesic domes amidst the Torres del Paine National Park in Patagonia, with a strong focus on sustainable and adventure tourism.

https://www.ecocamp.travel/

Four Seasons Tented Camp Golden Triangle – Thailand

A luxury tented camp offering unique experiences, such as elephant safaris and river cruises, in the heart of the Thai jungle.

https://www.fourseasons.com/goldentriangle/

Scarabeo Camp – Morocco

Luxury tents in the Moroccan desert offer a mix of adventure and comfort, with activities such as camel riding and stargazing.

https://www.scarabeocamp.com/

Galapagos Safari Camp – Ecuador

A luxury safari camp offering African tents with ocean views and a unique wildlife viewing experience in the Galapagos.

https://www.galapagossafaricamp.com/

Narrative Guest Experiences

As with the **Narrative Dinner Experience**, this type of receptive experience is characterized by a theme centered on a narrative linked to aspects such as: culture and traditions, knowledge and ancient crafts, myths and legends, natural aspects characterizing the territory, aspects linked to places of memory (historical, literary, filmic events, etc.).

Muraless Art Hotel

Hotel dedicated to the art of mural paintings; a real museum decorated by internationally renowned artists to celebrate Made in Italy.

https://www.itinerariesperienziali.it/en/directory-offerte/listing/muraless-art-hotel/

My Arbor Hotel

Entirely inspired by the beneficial charm of the forest.

https://www.itinerariesperienziali.it/en/directory-offerte/listing/my-arbor-hotel-bolzano/

The Wizarding World of Harry Potter – Universal Studios, Orlando, USA

Guests can experience the magic of the world of Harry Potter, with attractions, shops and restaurants inspired by the book and film series.

https://www.universalorlando.com/web/en/us/theme-parks/universal-studios-florida/the-wizarding-world-of-harry-potter-diagon-alley

Hobbiton Movie Set – Matamata, New Zealand

The world of "The Lord of the Rings" and "The Hobbit". Guests can explore replica Hobbit houses and other movie sets, as well as enjoy a feast at the Green Dragon Inn.

https://www.hobbitontours.com/

Ashford Castle – County Mayo, Ireland

Stay in a historic castle. Guests can live like nobility in an authentic castle, with activities like falconry and horseback riding.

https://ashfordcastle.com/

The Queen Mary – Long Beach, California, USA

Life aboard a historic ocean liner. Guests stay on a historic ocean liner, with tours and attractions that tell the story of the vessel.

https://queenmary.com/

3.3. Cultural Heritage Experience (CHE)

The experiences linked to visits to monuments and sites of cultural interest have as their main purpose the enjoyment of the Cultural Heritage and the immersion in the local lifestyle and in everything that constitutes its identity and character. Cultural heritage can be both material, such as monuments, historical and archaeological sites, and immaterial, such as festivals, traditions, local expressions and cultural events.

The **Cultural Heritage Experience** is often intertwined with the other types of experiences covered in this volume; therefore, a cultural experience can in many cases very well fit into other categories addressed.

Cultural Heritage Experiences include a vast range of experiences; a first classification, which inserts a further element of differentiation, could take into account the different possible narratives that concern one or more specific themes such as:

- **Food-and-Wine Experience:** The experience is mainly focused on aspects related to gastronomy or territorial events focused on local gastronomy (fairs, food festivals, etc.)
- **Location (Heritage Sides Experience):** The experience is particularly focused on visiting places of historical, archaeological, landscape and naturalistic interest. Visits to the villages and historic centers are included and places with national and international recognition (World Heritage Sites, Creative Cities, Capitals of Culture, etc.)
- **Intangible Cultural Heritage Experience:** The experience focuses on Intangible Cultural Heritage:
  - Culture and traditions
  - Artistic craftsmanship (Handmade Experience)
  - Ancient knowledge and crafts
  - Myths and legends
  - Aspects linked to places of memory (historical, religious, literary, filmic events, etc.)

- **Exhibition (Cultural Expositive Experience):** The experience focuses on exhibitions and exhibition events (painting, photography, art, museum and eco-museum installations, etc.). The following subclasses fall within this class:
  - Museum/Ecomuseum Experience
  - Immersive Art Experience
- **Entertainment (Cultural Entertainment Experience):** The experience focuses on events of a predominantly entertainment nature (theatrical, musical shows, games, etc.)
- **Learning (Cultural Learning Experience):** The experience is associated with forms of learning such as: typical local cuisine, artistic craftsmanship, or linked to school and educational visits, etc.
- **Interpretation of Cultural Heritage (Heritage Interpretation Experience):** The experience is based on the concept of Interpretation of cultural heritage and can be connected, from a thematic point of view, to the other types described.

The different thematic approaches are not necessarily different, as they are often present at the same time. In these cases, the prevailing approach is generally considered to be the primary approach and all others to be secondary.

An example: a guided tour that includes an experiential lunch linked to a specific historical event could simultaneously use different approaches: narrative, entertainment, exhibition, sensorial, and take place in the same location where the historical event that gave the inspiration took place to the experience you want to propose.

Within the Cultural Heritage Experiences, I would like to highlight two types of experiences linked to the exhibition approach, but as a strong connotation connected to the nature of the exhibition structure (museums and ecomuseums), mode and type of exhibition (immersive exhibitions) and aspects related to artistic craftsmanship.

A further type of experience that I wanted to highlight, falling within the **Intangible Cultural Experience**, is that linked to artistic craftsmanship (Handmade Experience).

The result is therefore that the following classification:

Cultural Heritage Experience (CHE)

- **Food and Wine Experience:** exploration and celebration of local food and wine.
- **Heritage Sides Experience:** visits and discoveries of places of historical, archaeological, landscape and natural interest and places with national and international recognition.
- **Intangible Cultural Heritage Experience:** experiences focused on intangible cultural heritage, including:
    - Handmade Experience: focused on artistic craftsmanship and manual skills.
- **Cultural Expositive Experience:** experiences related to exhibitions and exhibition events, with subcategories such as:
    - Museum/Ecomuseum experience: visits and interactions with museums and ecomuseums.
    - Immersive Art Experience: art exhibitions that offer an immersive experience to the visitor.
- **Cultural Entertainment Experience:** cultural events with a predominant element of entertainment.
- **Cultural Learning Experience:** experiences that provide learning opportunities.
- **Heritage Interpretation Experience:** experiences based on the concept of Cultural Heritage Interpretation.

For a formal definition of cultural heritage, we can refer to the definitions given in the Faro Convention and in the Recommendation concerning the protection and promotion of museums and collections, their diversity and their role in society adopted by UNESCO on 17 November 2015.

- **Cultural Heritage (Faro Convention)**

Cultural heritage is a set of assets inherited from the past that some people consider, regardless of the ownership regime of the assets, as a reflection and an expression of their constantly evolving values, beliefs, knowledge and traditions. It includes all aspects of the environment derived from the interaction between people and places over time.

- **Cultural Heritage (UNESCO 2015)**

A set of tangible and intangible values, and the expressions that people select and identify, independently of their ownership, as a reflection and expression of their identities, beliefs, knowledge and traditions, and living environments, worthy of protection and valorization by contemporary generations and to be passed on to generations.

Food and Wine Experience

The experience is mainly focused on aspects related to gastronomy or on events related to local food and wine.

Food and wine events have particular importance, in terms of integrated experiential service offerings, due to the fact that the role of food and wine in cultural tourism is increasingly central: 71% of people traveling want to have memorable food and wine experiences, while 59% of tourists say that themed experiences help them choose between multiple destinations. Food and wine experiences are more likely to be combined with other activities than generalist tourists, for example shopping (indicated by 85% versus 68% of generalist tourists) or music festivals (66% versus 45%). Tourists look for integrated proposals that combine a variety of food and wine themed experiences with other cultural and recreational activities. The "food trucks" - street food - are among the most experienced and most sought-after experiences on the web, the historic restaurants and bars and the historic homes home to agri-food production companies, the visits to non-wine producers, and finally the cuisine (Source: 2020 edition of the "Report on Italian Food and Wine Tourism" of the World Food Travel Association and the Italian Food and Wine Tourism Association).

Two specific cases must be distinguished:

- The experiential event consists mainly of a food and wine experience (experiential lunch)
- The lunch or food and wine tasting is a part that contributes to creating the guided tour.

As regards the first case, please refer to **Dinner Experiences**; in the second case the experience is linked not only to the food and wine aspect itself, but to the atmosphere and other aspects that are necessary for the experiential journey, often linked to the beauty and typical products of a territory. In these cases, it is appropriate to include elements that enrich the experience: the possibility of knowing the various phases of production or preparation of food, the possibility of directly participating in some phases of production or preparation of typical dishes, and other aspects that allow you to satisfy most of the experiential principles described.

Taste experiences along the Trentino Wine and Flavor Route

Taste&Train, Taste&Walk and Taste&Train are taste experiences of the Trentino Wine and Flavor Route, which includes a series of food and wine stops at the Route's members, which can be managed in total autonomy, to be reached thanks to practical and sustainable train journeys, on foot or by bike.

https://www.tastetrentino.it/le-tre-strade/strada-del-vino-e-dei-sapori-del-trentino/scoprire/esperienze/dettaglio-esperienza/p/taste-experience/

Napa Valley Wine Train – USA

A unique experience combining train travel, gourmet food and wine tastings through picturesque Napa Valley.

https://www.winetrain.com/

Fabiolous Food Tour

The **Fabiolous Food Tour** is a food and wine tour of Rome. Participants are accompanied on the less traveled routes of the city to experience the true flavors of Rome in the Trastevere district. During the tour, advice on Italian cuisine is provided and local food specialties are presented, in order to create an immersion in the rich culinary traditions of Rome. At the end of the culinary tour, participants will be able to drink wine and eat a dish of fresh pasta, prepared by one of the chefs from the team organizing the tour.

https://www.itinerariesperienziali.it/en/directory-offerte/listing/fabiolous-food-tour/

Cheese Tasting Tour in Switzerland

Tours exploring Swiss cheese production, with tastings and demonstrations.

https://www.swisstavolata.ch/

Truffle Hunting in France

Experiences that include searching for truffles with the help of expert truffle dogs and tastings of truffle-based dishes.

https://www.lespastras.com/

From the Garden to the Table. Among rows and scents of the vegetable gardens

For nature lovers and for those who wish to explore and taste authentic products and typical local recipes, a guided walk among the seasonal crops is proposed, which offers the discovery of a lesser-known aspect of the island territory.

During the experience, proceeding between rows and immersing yourself in the scents of the gardens, you will have the opportunity to meet fruit and vegetable producers, discovering their products, exploring their seasonality and learning the cultivation techniques, which, where possible, Traditional cultivation methods are applied.

https://www.itinerariesperienziali.it/en/directory-offerte/listing/dallorto-alla-tavola-tra-filari-e-profumi-degli-orti/

Heritage Sides Experience

This experience is particularly focused on visiting places of naturalistic, landscape, archaeological and historical-artistic interest. Also included are visits to villages, historic centers and places with national and international recognition, such as World Heritage Sites, Creative Cities, Capitals of Culture, etc.

Naturalistic experiences

If the interest is naturalistic, the aspects can also concern urban contexts and include parks, villas, monumental trees, botanical gardens, as well as urban treks. An example of this occurs in Rome, where city tours are organized that cross villas, parks and gardens, illustrating history, legends, curiosities and anecdotes about the precious vegetation of the Capital city of Italy.

When the environmental aspects are extra-urban, it might be more appropriate to talk about naturalistic excursions; in this case I refer to the Open-Air Experience.

Archaeological experiences

The archaeological experience is mainly focused on archaeological assets. In these cases, the visit should not be limited to the mere description of the archaeological heritage explored, but be enriched through the addition of tales, stories, legends and historical events. Where possible, it would also be useful to integrate practical demonstrations, directly involving participants. For example, if the archaeological site includes a place where grain was milled, it might be interesting to simulate grain milling in specially equipped areas. This would allow participants to 'travel through time', giving uniqueness to the experience.

As Tilden writes about an archaeological site where Indians milled grain:

«The visitor must have the impression that in the night, the ancient inhabitants of this archaeological site could return and regain possession, the grain will be ground again, the cries of children, of love and celebration will return. » (Freeman Tilden – Interpreting Heritage: Bringing the Past into the Present)

In essence, what we need to aim for within an experience is to carry out activities that in some way, as Tilden recalled in his book: 'bring the past to the present'.

Historical-artistic experiences

The historical-artistic experiences are mainly focused on visiting places of historical-artistic interest, villages and historic centers. What has already been indicated for archaeological visits applies: the visit should not be limited to the narration of the historical-artistic heritage, but it is necessary to enrich the visit with stories, legends, historical events and, where possible, also with practical demonstrations, possibly involving participants firsthand with animations and live demonstrations.

Rai 3.: Experiential tourism: working with your own history – The right place 17/12/2017

https://youtu.be/ySRW8e6An4E

Ontario Tourism Video Montage

https://youtu.be/077yuT2xew0

Bonaventure and his Treasures (Rome)

The experience consists of a visit to Complex of San Bonaventura on the Palatine, articulated in the knowledge of the Convent and the adjacent Church.

The Church preserves important paintings by Giovan Battista Bernaschi inside, while the external road that climbs from the Roman Forum towards the top of the Palatine is characterized by the Stations of the Cross, which recall the work of San Leonardo from Porto Maurizio, who here he studied and died at the end of his adventurous life, and to whom we owe the credit of having created the ceremony of the Via Crucis as it is still celebrated today. The visit also includes a brief stop in the convent environments such as the Sacristy, the Choir, the Refectory, and the small and secluded garden, which offers a spectacular view of the Palatine, the Celian and the Colosseum valley, as well as the meeting with a friar of the community who will talk about his life experience and the charitable and cultural works that are still carried out today by the friars of this community, following and in the spirit suggested by Saint Francis.

https://www.itinerariesperienziali.it/en/directory-offerte/listing/bonaventura-e-i-suoi-tesori/

Tramjazz – Rome

The experience offered by Tramjazz in Rome is unique and engaging. It combines an evening of live jazz music, a candlelit dinner and a tour of the center of Rome at night, all on board a historic tram, restored and transformed into a traveling restaurant and concert hall.

During the journey, the tram passes through various locations in Rome, including Piazza di Porta Maggiore, the Basilica of Santa Croce in Jerusalem, San Giovanni in Laterano Square, the Colosseum, the Circus Maximus, and the Pyramid of Cestius, offering participants the chance to admire these historical icons while enjoying music and dinner.

https://www.itinerariesperienziali.it/en/directory-offerte/listing/tramjazz-roma/

Petra, Jordan

Exploration of the city carved into the rock, with its history and its mysteries.

https://www.visitpetra.jo/

Machu Picchu, Peru

An adventure among the ruins of an ancient Inca city, immersed in an extraordinary naturalistic context.

https://www.machupicchu.gob.pe/

Alhambra, Granada, Spain

An experience that combines Moorish architecture, dazzling gardens and rich history.

https://www.alhambra-patronato.es/

Mill of the Ettore and Infersa saltpans

Salt tourism experiences offerings are of three types:

- **Walk in the salt pan**: The route is embellished by the changing colors of the pools, by the Stagnone Nature Reserve and by the accompaniment of the guides. During the itinerary, the complex life cycle and management of a salt pan will be illustrated, its production capacity, and the times and rhythms of salt harvesting.
- **Salinai by chance:** The profession of the Salinai, holders of an ancient centuries-old tradition handed down from father to son, represents an inestimable value. A historical and unique experience is offered, allowing you to transform into salt workers for a day. It is possible to enter and walk inside the tanks, photograph yourself among the white piles, use tools of the trade and participate in the harvest alongside the salt workers. The equipment, consisting of rubber boots and salt workers' tools, is made available on site.
- **Salt tasting:** Not all salts are the same and, consequently, taste and use vary. This experience allows you to get to know all the salts, obtained and collected by hand from the salt pans, and you are sure to be surprised both by the different flavors that you will notice and by their unique characteristics. Under the expert guidance of the selmeliers, you will discover the different types of salts, from *wholemeal* to *fleur de sel*, and the differences with other qualities of salt from other parts of the world.

https://www.itinerariesperienziali.it/en/directory-offerte/listing/mulino-delle-saline-ettore-e-infersa/

Intangible Cultural Heritage Experience

This experience focuses on **Intangible Cultural Heritage**. What has already been indicated several times applies: it is necessary to enrich visits on cultural events linked to intangible heritage with storytelling and activities that delve deeper into the topics covered by the visit; obviously, where possible, also with practical demonstrations, possibly involving participants personally with animations and live demonstrations.

Chongqing Intangible Cultural Heritage Experience Center

The Chongqing Experience Center for Intangible Cultural Heritage is a place that celebrates and showcases a wide range of cultural and creative products related to intangible cultural heritage. Some examples of products on display:

- **Chongqing Impression:** works created using the *paper-cutting* technique, a traditional Chinese art that involves cutting pieces of paper into artistic designs using scissors or knives, are presented. This art form is often used to create decorations, express greetings during the holidays and, occasionally, to tell stories through the silhouettes created.
- **Seventeen Gates of Chongqing Pyrography:** on display are works created using the pyrography technique, the art which consists of decorating wood or other materials with burn marks, obtained by applying a heated object, such as a metal tip, in a controlled manner.

https://www.ichongqing.info/culture/cultural-heritage/chongqing-intangible-cultural-heritage-experience-center/

La Diada de Sant Jordi – Barcelona, Spain

A party that celebrates love, culture and literature, where men give a rose to women and women give a book to men, with events, readings and activities throughout the city.

https://www.barcelonaturisme.com/wv3/en/

Holi Festival – India

Also known as the 'festival of colors', Holi is a lively festival that celebrates the arrival of spring with music, dancing and, of course, the throwing of colored powders.

https://www.holifestival.org/

Gion Matsuri – Kyoto, Japan

One of Japan's oldest and most famous festivals, the Gion Matsuri takes place in July and features float processions, traditional events and activities.

https://www.insidekyoto.com/

Learn to dance the Apulian pizzica

Guests will have the opportunity to learn about the history of Apulian popular music and *tarantism*, a social phenomenon linked to popular music, which characterized Southern Italy until the middle of the last century. Afterwards, a workshop is planned, during which guests will learn the traditional Apulian pizzica, starting from the basic steps of the traditional dance and moving following the rhythm of the drum and accordion. The experience will end with a convivial moment, during which a tasting of a typical Apulian aperitif will be offered among the *trulli*, based on wine, *friselle*, cheeses and seasonal fruit.

https://www.itinerariesperienziali.it/en/directory-offerte/listing/impara-a-ballare-la-pizzica-pugliese/

Cultural Expositive Experience

This experience focuses on exhibitions and exhibition events.

Museum/Ecomuseum Experience

In relation to the type of involvement of the participants, the objectives and the (eco)museum theme, an (eco)museum can carry out many of the activities listed below (partial and non-exhaustive list):

- Exhibition and museum activities (indoors and outdoors)
    - Museum and ecomuseum installations in general
    - In situ activities that reproduce parts of product production/processing of products
    - Reconstruction of environments intended for the production/processing of products
    - Reconstruction of rural environments
    - Reconstruction of environments linked to popular traditions
    - Reconstruction of environments linked to historical events
    - Reconstruction of environments linked to industrial archaeology
    - Reconstruction of environments linked to classical archaeology
- Teaching and training activities in the laboratory
- Field teaching and training activities
- Tastings of typical products
- Direct participation in some production/work phases related to the products
- Direct participation in some phases related to the preparation of food and wine recipes
- Guided visits and walks to the production sites
- Nature walks
- Cultural visits in urban, archaeological, historical-artistic environments
- Guided visits to places of remembrance
    - Places of Myth and Legends
    - Places of the Sacred

    - Places of historical events
    - Places of historical personalities and culture
    - Historical places of work
    - Historic places of taste
    - Places of the literary, television and filmic tale
    - Places of ancient communities
- Playful and recreational activities linked to aspects considered cultural identities
- Holidays, Celebrations and Ritual Practices
    - Holidays (sacred and profane)
    - Celebrations
    - Rites and Ritual Practices (urban and rural)
- Popular Expressions and Stories
    - Dialects, Speech and Jargons
    - Dances, Music and Songs (including songs of the cycle of life and the year (lullabies, nursery rhymes, etc.)
    - Poems (popular and religious)
    - Performing Arts (including plays)
- Uses, Customs and Beliefs
    - Games and Pastimes
    - Popular beliefs
    - Folk medicine
- Other local entertainment activities

Therefore, a museum/ecomuseum experience could also be structured and include one or more of the activities described.

ArtScience Museum Singapore

This museum uses art to explore science and our relationship with it. Large, immersive installations invite visitors to examine their relationship with the physical world around them. The permanent exhibition **Future World** shows how the slightest human interaction with the planet can change the environment, with projections of natural environments that respond to visitors' movements.

https://www.tiqets.com/blog/interactive-museum/

The Museum of Ice Cream, Various locations (USA)

The museum offers an interactive experience that celebrates ice cream in all its forms. Each room offers a different experience, often with opportunities to indulge in sweets along the way.

https://www.museumoficecream.com/

The Exploratorium, San Francisco, USA

The Exploratorium is a science, technology and art museum where you can create your own experiences through hundreds of interactive exhibits.

https://www.exploratorium.edu/

The National Museum of Mathematics (MoMath), New York, USA

The MoMath Museum seeks to improve public understanding of mathematics through dynamic and interactive activities. Exhibitions that allow visitors to experience mathematics in new and unexpected ways, such as **Math Square**, a luminous floor that reacts to foot movements.

https://momath.org/

Wool Art Museum

A guided tour with sensory experiences.

https://www.itinerariesperienziali.it/en/directory-offerte/listing/museo-dell-arte-della-lana/

Ecomuseum of Straw in the peasant tradition

In Crosara, this Ecomuseum was established to document how, in these hills, the tradition of straw processing, in particular braiding (*dressa*), was consolidated. High quality bags and hats were produced using this technique, contributing to the development of a prosperous industry, until the market moved towards more modern materials. The museum houses a vast collection of artefacts, skillfully made by women expert in the use of *fastughi*, stems derived from a particular type of wheat. These hills, thanks to their conformation and the composition of the soil, were able to produce ductile and malleable stems. A market system has developed around this domestic production which, unfortunately, has highlighted the exploitation of women's work. The exhibition also illustrates the production of cherries, present in high quality varieties.

https://www.itinerariesperienziali.it/en/directory-offerte/listing/ecomuseo-della-paglia-nella-tradizione-contadina/

Immersive Art Experience

Immersive Art Experiences represent artistic experiences that make use of advanced technologies and creative approaches in order to completely immerse visitors in art. These experiences go beyond the traditional observation of works of art in a gallery, actively engaging the visitor's senses and, in some instances, allowing them to become part of the work itself.

We have already seen some examples in relation to the experiential principle of *immersion*, just two further examples to follow.

GENIUS Da Vinci Immersive Experience

https://youtu.be/zdcb-4MNJRo

Macbeth Immersive Experience

https://youtu.be/z3GELMODj1c

Cultural Entertainment Experience

The experience focuses on events of a predominantly entertainment nature (theatrical, musical shows, games, etc.)

Augenblick

It is an immersive theater at the Studio Uno Theater in Rome, therefore it offers an immersive theatrical experience in which spectators have the opportunity to lose themselves in the plot, becoming active characters and at the same time users of the theatrical performance.

https://youtu.be/LOzZtIXcd7E?si=UF6bR01P5xJ-nY-3

The Globe Theatre, London, England

This theater offers performances of the works of William Shakespeare, maintaining style and atmosphere as faithful as possible to the Elizabethan era.

https://www.shakespearesglobe.com/

Luau, Hawaii, USA

Traditional Hawaiian celebrations that combine food, music and dance to offer a unique and authentic cultural experience.

https://oldlahainaluau.com/

Kabuki Theatre, Tokyo, Japan

Kabuki theater performances, a traditional Japanese art form that combines drama, dance and musical skills.

https://www.kabukiweb.net/

Cultural Tour to Kinigi (Rwanda)

Thanks to the presence of expert instructors, each participant can have fun learning traditional drums and dances. The cultural entertainment experience begins with a mini performance by a small troupe of local artists. Afterwards, the user is offered the opportunity to wear a traditional costume and try it on. Fun is guaranteed as the dancers teach some basic dance steps and share some of the history of Rwandan dance. After some practice, expert dance instructors assist in putting it all together into a personal performance.

https://www.itinerariesperienziali.it/en/directory-offerte/listing/tour-culturale-a-kinigi-ruanda/

Cultural Learning Experience

Experience that focuses on learning and discovering cultural, historical, artistic or artisanal aspects of a particular place or community. This type of experience can take different forms and can be structured in different ways, depending on the cultural context in which it is offered.

Here are some operational applications, from which it immediately emerges that this type of experience also falls into other experiential categories. Including it also within the Cultural Learning Experience intends to underline the aspect of cultural learning intrinsic to the experience itself:

- **Language and culture courses:** lessons that offer immersion in the local language and culture, often combined with hands-on activities and guided tours.
- **Historical and Cultural Guided Tours**: tours that offer insights into history, art, architecture and cultural heritage, often with access to sites and places of particular interest.
- **Traditional Music and Dance Workshop**: practical lessons where participants can learn dances or musical instruments typical of the local culture.
- **Archaeological or Historical Fields**: experiences that allow you to participate in archaeological excavations or restoration projects, offering a practical and theoretical understanding of historical and archaeological processes.
- **Cultural or Spiritual Retreats**: Retreats that offer immersion in spiritual or meditative practices, often in places of cultural or spiritual significance.
- **Local Cuisine Workshop**: Participants can learn to prepare traditional dishes, using local ingredients and cooking techniques.
- **Craft workshops**: Activities may include the creation of typical handicrafts, such as pottery, weaving, woodworking, etc., under the guidance of local artisans.

British Museum – London, UK

The **British Museum** offers workshops and learning sessions for schools and teachers, providing resources and activities that explore world history and cultures through objects in the museum's collection.

https://www.britishmuseum.org/learn/schools

The Metropolitan Museum of Art – New York City, USA

The Met offers educational programs and resources for students, teachers, and adults, including workshops, classes, and tours that explore art and culture across its vast collections.

https://www.metmuseum.org/learn/kids-and-families

The National Museum of Anthropology – Mexico City, Mexico

The museum offers educational programs and activities that explore the rich history and culture of Mexico, through its collections of art and archaeological artifacts.

https://www.mna.inah.gob.mx/

The Acropolis Museum – Athens, Greece

The Acropolis Museum explores the ancient history and culture of Greece through its collections and archaeological finds.

https://www.theacropolismuseum.gr/en

Heritage Interpretation Experience

I refer to my book "Experiential Paths and Interpretation of Cultural Heritage Vol. 1: Origins and Theoretical Principles [6]" for further information on the concept of Interpretation of Cultural Heritage; here I will limit myself to providing the information necessary to make it clear that a journey of interpretation of cultural heritage is to all intents and purposes an experiential journey, which fully falls within the possible tourist choices, and therefore deserves its own specific classification.

Let's start with some definitions given to the following word:

Interpretation

«Educational activity which aspires to reveal meanings and relationships through the use of original objects, experiences to live in first person and exemplary means, rather than the mere transmission of facts. [7]» (Freeman Tilden – 1957)

«Interpretation is a communication process, designed for reveal meanings and relationships of our cultural and natural heritage, through engagement with objects, artifacts, landscapes and sites. [8]» (the Canadian Interpretation Association – 1976)

Cultural experience, hermeneutics e systemic which aims at reveal the deeper meaning of things object of interpretation. (Ignazio Caloggero 2022)

---

[6] Ignazio Caloggero - Percorsi Esperienziali e Interpretazione del Patrimonio Culturale Vol. 1: Origini e Principi Teorici - Centro Studi Helios 2022

[7] Freeman Tilden: Interpretare il nostro patrimonio – Edizione italiana del 2019 – Libreria Geografica p. 29

[8] https://www.heritagedestination.com/hdc-training---what-is-heritage-interpretation/

The 18 Principles of Interpretation

1. **Multisensory Approach**: the interpretation must be multi-sensory as much as possible (involvement of at least two or more senses: sight, hearing, touch, smell, taste)
2. **Cultural Approach (Local Identities)**: the interpretation must allow to deepen the knowledge of elements of local identity
3. **Uniqueness**: the interpreting experience path must have characteristics of uniqueness
4. **Centrality of the participants**: each interpretation must take into account the participants and take into account their centrality with respect to the context
5. **Participation**: the interpreting experience path must foresee the participation, possibly direct, of the guest in the activities
6. **Educational Process (Experiential Learning)**: interpreting must include an experiential learning phase
7. **Thematic approach**: each interpretation it will have to be built starting from a theme that characterizes it and that constitutes its guiding thread.
8. **Aesthetic approach**: the aesthetic approach is one of the elements, together with that of direct participation, at the basis of the concept of *immersion*. The events that constitute 'the staging of the experience' must be designed in such a way as to give importance to all aspects that can influence aesthetics: the atmosphere, the sense of beauty, the place chosen for the experience, the plot (screenplay) which must be consistent with the chosen theme and the identified location
9. **Entertainment**: each Interpretation Experience path should also include moments of entertainment that enrich and make the experience pleasant
10. **Immersion**: the principle of immersion, as well as in experiential paths, is the direct consequence of the application of the principles of multisensory, direct participation and aesthetic approach
11. **Revelation (hermeneutical communication)**: interpretation is a hermeneutic communication process (whether art or discipline), which aims to reveal the

deepest meaning of things. The revelation occurs through the transformation of the personal interpretative experience lived by the visitor

12. **Provocation (communication based on provocation)**: the communicative process that allows the interpreter to reveal (not teach) and the participant of the experience to discover (not learn) occurs thanks to the provocation, on the part of the interpreter, of the curiosity and involvement of the participants.
13. **Systemic approach (holistic view)**: the interpretation must take place with a holistic approach, it should take into account all aspects, the relationships and links between the participants, the good (or phenomenon) interpreted and the context in which the three elements underlying the interpretation are found. interpretation: the interpreter, the good (or phenomenon) and the participant.
14. **Tailored approach**: the interpretation must take into account both the target of the final users: age, education, social context, and other variables such as expressed and implicit needs of the users themselves. For each target identified, specific themes, methods and programs must be identified
15. **Creative approach**: the interpretation process must precede a communicative style that must involve the whole dynamic of thought, describing places and facts in a creative and engaging way and using interpretative techniques such as storytelling and creative writing
16. **Interpretation based on facts**: interpretation must originally have concrete facts and places. The information on which the interpretation is based must be based on in-depth and quality data and information
17. **Simplicity and communicative coherence**: interpretation must include language that is not overly technical, lengthy or irrelevant to the context to be interpreted
18. **Emotional connection (passion)**: the interpreter must love the object of the interpretation; the result of the same is strongly correlated to the passion and emotional connection that binds the interpreter and the phenomenon to be interpreted.

In relation to the principles of interpretation, we could classify three levels, and consequently three further levels of experiences of interpretation of Cultural Heritage:

- Simple interpretation (first level): application of principles 1, 2, 3, 11, 12, 13, 16
- Authentic interpretation (second level): application of principles 1, 2, 3, 4, 5, 6, 7, 11, 12, 13, 16
- Full interpretation (third level): application of principles 1, 2, 3, 4, 5, 6, 7, 8, 9, 10, 11, 12, 13, 14, 15, 16, 17, 18

A definition of the three levels of interpretation that takes into account the applied principles could be the following:

- **Simple interpretation (first level)**

  Interpretation of cultural heritage which aims, through a holistic approach, to reveal the deepest meaning of things through a unique, multi-sensory communication process based on provocation and the validity of facts.

- **Authentic interpretation (second level)**

  Interpretation of cultural heritage that aims, through a holistic approach, to reveal the deepest meaning of things through a multi-sensory, unique, thematic communicative process, based on provocation, substantiation of facts, human relationships and direct participation of guests' participants in the activities that constitute the interpretive experience.

- **Full interpretation (third level)**

  Interpretation of cultural heritage which aims, through a creative, holistic, aesthetic, immersive and tailor-made approach, to reveal the deepest meaning of things through a multi-sensory, unique, thematic, coherent communication process, based on provocation, factual basis, relationships humans and direct participation of the guests' participants in the activities, including entertainment, that constitute the interpretive experience.

As you can see, the first ten principles are nothing more than the principles of the experiential path.

An **Interpretation Path** is an experiential path (not the other way around) and is made up of a purely experiential component (principles 1 to 10) and a purely interpretative component (principles 11 to 18).

The purely interpretative components alone are not enough to create an interpretative path: the experiential components must always also be applied.

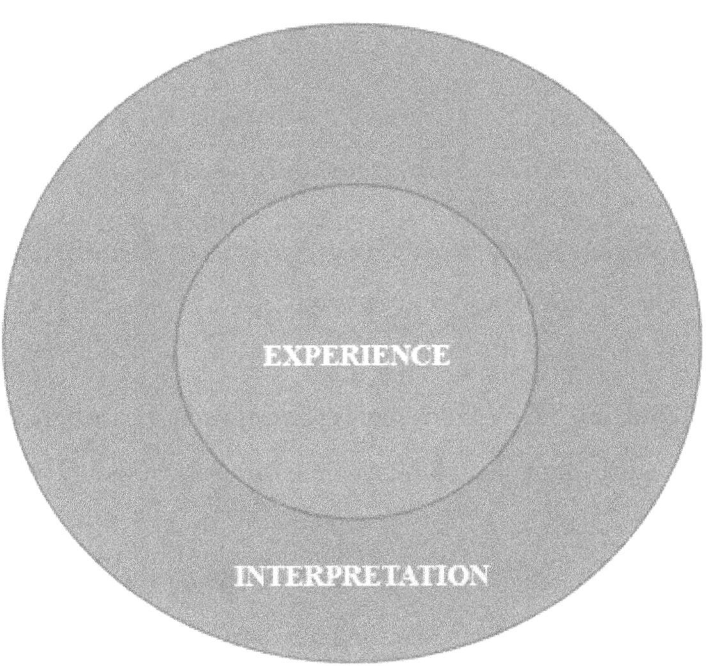

Heritage Interpretation Experience Centers (CEIP)

The term **Interpretation Center (CIP)** has been used for some time in the field of cultural heritage interpretation. The definition I prefer to use, which in essence does not differ much from the former, is **Interpretation Experience Center (CEIP)**, as it underlines the importance that the center has in offering what are indicated here as **Paths of Interpretation Experience.**

Another reason that pushes me to use the term CEIP is that often the CIPs (as well as some ecomuseums), which define themselves as such, do not always respect, or respect only minimally, the principles that underlie of interpretation. In some cases, the very definition of CIP refers to simple museum institutions.

In relation to the principles of interpretation we could classify three types of CEIP corresponding to the three levels of interpretation previously illustrated:

- **CEIP-I (Centre of First Level Heritage Interpretation Experiences)**: Center that respects the principles of interpretation for simple interpretation (1, 2, 3, 11, 12, 13, 16)
- **CEIP-II (Second level Heritage Interpretation Experience Center)**: Center that respects the principles of interpretation for authentic interpretation (1, 2, 3, 4, 5, 6, 7, 11, 12, 13, 16)
- **CEIP-III (Third level Heritage Interpretation Experience Center)**: Center that respects the principles of interpretation for full interpretation (1, 2, 3, 4, 5, 6, 7, 8, 9, 10, 11, 12, 13, 14, 15, 16, 17, 18).

To be considered a CEIP it is therefore sufficient to respect the principles established for the first level of interpretation (simple interpretation).

Principle no.18 is not always easily detectable through objective evidence, but it should be taken for granted that at the basis of everything there must be a strong emotional connection, which binds the CEIP actors with the cultural heritage being interpreted. Therefore, this indicator, unless objective evidence demonstrates the contrary, is taken as applied.

Who can be CEIP

Museums, Ecomuseums, Parks and Nature Reserves, Laboratories and Educational Centers, Visitors Centers, Educational Farms, structures for organizing artistic or cultural experiential events, other territorial structures in possession of the minimum requirements for first level CEIPs.

Integral Museum of the Laguna Blanca Biosphere Reserve

The **Laguna Blanca Integral Museum** extends within the limits of the **Biosphere Reserve** itself, therefore covering an area of 455.400 hectares and integrating several villages and habitats scattered across the territories of the 5 local indigenous communities. In all aspects of the work carried out, the Museum team engages in socially useful science, supporting local indigenous communities in the processes they are going through, participating in research on the regional past and recovering invisible local history. This territory, inhabited for millennia by women, men and children, is witness to multiple experiences and knowledge, of forgetfulness, struggles and resistance.

Among the various activities linked to the concept of interpretation, the museum has activated the following:

- a reception and interpretation center (CRI),
- Archaeological Museums of the Site,
- an Andean botanical park called 'Paul Günther Lorentz',
- a circuit through sites with rock art (pictograms and petroglyphs),
- some panoramic interpretation sites (SiPI),
- an interpretative trail of the *quirquincho*,
- an experimental plot of native Andean crops,
- a Huaraco-type Andean greenhouse.

https://www.itinerariesperienziali.it/en/directory-offerte/listing/museo-integral-de-la-reserva-de-biosfera-de-laguna-blanca/

Ecomuseu de Maranguape

The **Maranguape Ecomuseum**, centered on the new museology movement, no longer places the object at the center, but the subject: the community and its cultural and territorial heritage, at the service of local development. With 1500 inhabitants, of which 400 under the age of 18, the initiative has taught the municipality of Cachoeira to grow. The Ecomuseum has broadened the community's horizons by changing belief systems and strengthening cultural and popular identity. The project's collection, curated by residents and students, evolves through research. The mansion houses photos and artifacts, while outside visitors explore the natural history of *Cachoeira*. There are workshops on cultural heritage, craftsmanship and permaculture, and the *Festa do Feijão Verde* is celebrated annually, a tribute to local cuisine and poetry.

https://www.itinerariesperienziali.it/en/directory-offerte/listing/ecomuseu-de-maranguape/

3.4. Open-Air Experience (OAE)

This is an experience in close contact with nature or outdoors, and it is also known by the term **Outdoor Experience**.

Open-Air Experiences can offer a variety of activities and are often customizable to participants' preferences and abilities. These experiences allows the user to connect with nature, explore unique environments, and participate in activities that can be both relaxing and adventurous. Furthermore, Open-Air Experiences can also be combined with local cultural, historical or gastronomic elements, creating a complete and engaging tourist experience.

Open-Air Experiences can therefore include a wide range of activities, such as:

- **Trekking and Hiking Experience:** exploration of natural paths and routes through walking or hiking.
- **Bike Experience:** cycle routes and bike tours through different types of landscapes.
- **Diving Experience:** underwater exploration of coral reefs, shipwrecks and other underwater wonders.
- **Speleology Experience:** exploration of caves and underground cavities.
- **River Experience:** experience linked to various activities or initiatives characterized by a river aspect, which may include nature excursions along rivers, wildlife observation, and visits to historical or cultural sites along the river.
- **Horse Experience:** horseback riding through various terrains and landscapes.
- **Donkey Experience:** walking and trekking in the company of donkeys, often used to carry luggage.
- **Animal Experience:** interactions and observations of wildlife in a natural environment.
- **Marine Life Experience:** exploration of marine life through snorkeling, diving or boat trips.
- **Flight Experience:** flight experiences

- **Fishing Tourism Experience:** fishing experiences which may include participation in traditional fishing activities.

Glamping Experiences and, in some cases, **Farmhouse Experiences**, are to be considered **Open-Air Experiences**, although in the repertoire of experiential activities 1.2, for practical reasons and to emphasize the aspect linked to hospitality, they have been included within the category **Guest Experience**. A similar argument applies to **Sport Experiences**, particularly for those sports in direct contact with nature, for which there is currently its own category. The Open-Air Experience however maintains close contacts with many other open field experiences included in other categories, such as **Dinner Experience** in the trees or amid nature, **Cultural Heritage Experience** and **Wellness Experience** in naturalistic sites, etc.

Trekking and Hiking Experience

The **Trekking and Hiking Experience** represents an activity that allows you to immerse oneself in nature, explore landscapes and, in some cases, undertake a spiritual journey. This type of experience can vary greatly depending on the location, the difficulty of the route and the objectives of the trip.

Below is a non-exhaustive list of typical activities related to **Trekking and Hiking Experience**:

Exploration and Adventure

- **Discovery of Nature:** exploration of various ecosystems, from the mountains to the forest, passing through paths and natural routes.
- **Wildlife Watching:** observation of wildlife in its natural habitat during the route.
- **Photography:** Capture breathtaking moments and views along the way.

Spiritual and Religious Paths

- **Santiago's walk:** a route that crosses Spain, known for its spiritual and religious connotations.
- **Via Francigena**: an ancient pilgrimage route that leads to Rome, crossing various Italian regions and European countries.
- **Walks in Japan:** like the Kumano Kodo and the 88 Temples Walk of Shikoku, which offer a unique spiritual and cultural experience.

Culture and History

- **Historical Routes:** Exploring trails that have historical significance, such as the Via dell'Amicizia in the Dolomites or the Freedom Trail in the USA.
- **Cultural Trekking:** Routes that cross archaeological sites, ancient villages and places of cultural interest.

Environmental education

- **Educational Trekking:** guided excursions with a focus on environmental education and knowledge of flora and fauna.
- **Field Workshop:** educational activities and practical workshops on topics such as survival in nature, orientation or photography.

Wildland Trekking

Wildland Trekking offers a variety of trekking and hiking experiences, including guided tours, backpacking excursions, and multi-day trips to diverse destinations around the world, such as Alaska, the Alps, Bryce Canyon, Grand Canyon, and many more.

https://wildlandtrekking.com/

Wilderness Travel

Wilderness Travel offers a range of hiking and trekking tours to several global destinations, including the Alps, New Zealand, Patagonia, Himalayas, Peru, Kilimanjaro, Italy, and the United Kingdom. Trips are designed for those who prefer an energetic excursion rather than a scenic journey, and are led by industry experts.

https://www.wildernesstravel.com/hiking-trekking/

REI Adventures

REI Adventures offers a wide range of trekking and hiking tours around the world, including trips to destinations such as Machu Picchu, Tanzania, Greece, and many US national parks. It also offers options for various skill levels and interests, including families, women, and solo travelers.

https://www.rei.com/adventures

G adventures

G Adventures offers a variety of trekking experiences that take travelers to adventure destinations around the world. Options include the following: trekking through the Andes Mountains to reach Machu Picchu, exploring the Himalayan trails, and much more. The itineraries are designed to offer a mix of adventure, culture, and nature.

https://www.gadventures.com/

The Via Francigena at sunset

Short trek in search of the most beautiful panoramic points of Castelnuovo d'Elsa, where you can admire the sunset. The excursion, according to what can be read on the organizers' website, is also an opportunity to learn about some historical curiosities of this ancient village and the difficult life of the pilgrim.

https://www.toscanahiking.it/events/francigena-tramonto-071023/

Bike Experience

Bike Experience is configured as an experience that allows you to cross landscapes, cities and territories using bikes, offering an experience that is both active and frequently immersive, both from a naturalistic and cultural point of view. This experience, by virtue of its nature, can show notable variations in terms of duration, degree of difficulty and theme.

Bike Experiences can embrace a variety of aspects and facets, including:

- **Naturalistic Cycling Routes:** exploration of parks, nature reserves, or characteristic landscapes through paths and routes dedicated to bicycles.
- **Urban Cycle Tours:** routes through cities and urban centers, often with a guide who shares historical and cultural information about the places visited.
- **Bikepacking:** a form of cycle tourism that combines mountain biking with self-managed camping.
- **Food and wine tours by bicycle:** itineraries that combine cycling exploration with local food and wine tastings.
- **Thematic Routes:** itineraries that follow a specific theme, such as historical, religious, or literary routes, exploring related places and stories.

Trek Travel Bike Trips

Trek Travel has been offering cycling experiences around the world for more than 20 years. It offers luxurious cycling trips in Europe and adventurous tours through national parks, with various options for every type of cyclist.

https://trektravel.com/

Backroads Bike Tours

They have been offering bike tours since they were founded in 1979. Their bike tours have been perfected with decades of experience, offering routes ranging from the Rocky Mountains to the Tuscan countryside to the rural villages of Vietnam.

https://www.backroads.com/award-winning-tours/biking

Cycling for gourmets in the Lower Parma area

Crossing the land of Giuseppe Verdi offers the discovery of its typical products, proposing a safe route that offers an authentic experience in an area of extraordinary musical and food and wine culture.

Participation involves cycling through the Lower Parma area, accompanied by a professional who combines the skills of a chef, gastronome, tour leader and environmental hiking guide, with a particular specialization in food and wine cycle tourism.

https://www.itinerariesperienziali.it/en/directory-offerte/listing/pedalata-per-buongustai-nella-bassa-parmense/

Diving Experience

Diving Experience is an underwater adventure that allows participants to explore the underwater world, offering a unique experience. This type of experience can include exploring coral reefs, shipwrecks, underwater caves and the chance to observe marine life up close. Diving experiences can vary greatly depending on location and the specific underwater attractions available.

Diving Experiences can explore a variety of elements and features, including the following:

- **Wreck Exploration:** dives that take place in places characterized by the presence of shipwrecks, airplanes or submerged buildings, providing an adventure that is intertwined with history.
- **Coral reefs:** diving in areas where coral reefs are prevalent, offering a visual spectacle of exceptional beauty linked to marine fauna and coral structures.
- **Underwater life:** close observation of various species that populate the seas, such as fish, corals, mollusks and, in certain locations, even sharks and rajiformes.
- **Exploration of Caves and Underwater Caverns:** the investigation of underwater geological formations, caves and caverns, offering a unique and often exciting experience.
- **Underwater photography:** for photography enthusiasts, diving represents an opportunity to immortalize extraordinary underwater scenery, capturing the life and scenery of the deep.
- **Marine Preservation:** some diving experiences are also related to conservation initiatives, offering divers the opportunity to actively participate in safeguarding marine ecosystems.

Sardine Run, South Africa

From May to July, almost every year, millions of sardines travel along the east coast of South Africa. Dolphins herd sardines, while sharks, whales, seabirds, penguins and seals dive in, feasting on the small fish. Diving excursions depart from several locations in South Africa and can last up to seven hours, with sightings of schools of sardines every few days.

https://blog.padi.com/worlds-most-epic-dive-trips/

Pemba Island, the untold story

With the use of a speed boat, it is possible to quickly visit the 25 dive sites on the north-west coast of Pemba. Each dive site can be adapted to different levels of diving experience, accommodating both novice individuals and experienced divers. Tropical reef systems pronounced underwater walls and tidal currents, which attract pelagic fish, give Pemba a reputation as a premier diving destination.

https://www.itinerariesperienziali.it/en/directory-offerte/listing/pemba-island-the-untold-story/

Diving Experience in Portorotondo

The opportunity to experience scuba diving is offered for those who have never tried it, but want to explore the underwater world and swim among fish. During this Diving Experience it will be possible to experiment with the use of diving equipment, always under the supervision of qualified instructors. After a short briefing on the basic rules of diving, we will proceed with the dive in the clear waters of *Cala dei Sardi*. Every detail will be managed by the organization; the only requirement for participants is to bring a swimsuit and join the group.

https://www.itinerariesperienziali.it/en/directory-offerte/listing/diving-experience-a-portorotondo/

Speleology Experience

Exploration of caves and underground cavities. Also known as **Caving Experience**.

Speleology experiences can present various degrees of complexity, ranging from easily navigable caves and well-lit itineraries, also suitable for families and beginners, up to more technical and demanding routes that require specific equipment and a certain mastery of speleological techniques.

Some focal elements of caving adventures may include:

- **Exploration:** the investigation of underground environments and the observation of singular geological formations.
- **Adventure:** undertake physical challenges such as climbing, crawling, and occasionally swimming.
- **Education:** learning about the geology, ecology and history of caves.
- **Food container:** acquire awareness of the importance of protecting caves and underground ecosystems.

Caving experiences can also provide historical and archaeological insight, as some caves have been used by humans for millennia and house ancient artifacts and wall art.

Speleology – Grand Pic Saint-Loup tourist office

The experience includes rope descents, discovery of large chambers, particular geological formations and *subterranean landscapes.*

https://www.grandpicsaintloup-tourisme.fr/en/speleology

Speleology Full day – Cave of Castelette – Plan-d'Aups-Sainte-Baume

This experience offers the chance to explore the **Cave of Castelette**. This cave, carved by the underground river of *Huveaune*, allows you to discover beautiful tunnels and descend to admire the wonders that these cavities offer.

https://www.marseille-tourisme.com/en/experience/speleology-full-day-cave-of-castelette-plan-daups-sainte-baume-en-3833818/

Speleology – Cave of Mons

An adventure into the depths of underground caves, which, combining playful and educational elements, reveals an extraordinarily preserved world, rich in mineral, aquatic and biological elements. The exploration activity proposes an approach that combines scientific and educational aspects relating to caves.

The opportunity is offered to learn to identify stalactites, stalagmites and drapery, as well as to interpret the colors associated with the different observable minerals.

https://www.itinerariesperienziali.it/en/directory-offerte/listing/speleology-cave-of-mons/

Speleology experience in Garfagnana

A captivating excursion reveals the secrets of the underground world, guiding participants along an underground waterway and through environments adorned with thousand-year-old concretions. The presence of stalactites and stalagmites, which occasionally merge into astonishing columns of calcium carbonate of unimaginable dating, transforms the visit into a genuine experience. The use of wetsuits facilitates passage under waterfalls and, if desired, it is possible to immerse oneself in a crystal-clear underground lake.

If desired, you can experience a short walk through narrow passages, followed by a visit to the silence room, where you experience total darkness.

https://www.itinerariesperienziali.it/en/directory-offerte/listing/esperienza-di-speleologia-a-garfagnana/

River Experience

This experience is linked to various activities or initiatives characterized by the river aspect; and may include nature hikes along rivers, wildlife viewing, as well as visits to historic or cultural sites along the river.

They can include sporting activities such as rafting, kayaking and fishing which offer unique ways to experience the river and the surrounding landscape or simply peaceful boat trips.

River Experiences may also include educational programs and activities, or environmental interpretation, to educate visitors about river ecology, conservation, and the importance of river systems.

For some of the activities described, River Experiences can therefore also be configured as **Sport Experiences**.

Ocoee River | Ocoee River Experience

Ocoee River Experience is a rafting company on the Ocoee River. It also offers off-water activities for all ages, a full-service restaurant, and can accommodate large and small groups, as well as families, with various lodging options and amenities.

https://theocoeeriver.com/rafting-company/ocoee-river-experience/

The River Experience (London)

The River Experience in London offers several opportunities to explore the city from a unique and compelling perspective, sailing across the River *Thames*, a river that flows through the heart of London and has long been used as a commercial artery.

https://www.itinerariesperienziali.it/en/directory-offerte/listing/the-river-experience-london/

River Trekking Experience

This experience is also classifiable as **Trekking Experience**. River Trekking consists of excursions where you alternate sections in the woods with sections directly walking in the water. The location is that of the **Pollino National Park**, which extends into Basilicata and Calabria.

https://www.itinerariesperienziali.it/en/directory-offerte/listing/river-trekking-experience/

Horse Experience

These are experiences related to horseback riding through various terrains and landscapes.

Horse Experiences offer a unique way to explore nature and landscapes, allowing participants to connect with animals and nature, while interacting with the world around them.

Horse Experiences can also offer a wide range of benefits, including physical and mental wellbeing and learning new skills.

Some focal elements of horseback riding experiences may include:

- **Horse excursions:** guided walks through different environments, such as beaches, mountains, forests or countryside.
- **Horse Safari:** exploring wildlife and natural ecosystems from a unique perspective.
- **Horse riding lessons:** training sessions that can cover the fundamental elements of horsemanship, horse care, or specific riding styles such as dressage or jumping.
- **Hippotherapy:** using horses as a means to provide physical and psychological therapy.
- **Equestrian Camps and Retreats:** immersive experiences that can last several days and include a variety of horse-related activities.
- **Historical or Thematic Horseback Riding Excursions:** equestrian itineraries that follow historical routes or are organized around a particular theme.

Equitours

Equitours offers diverse equestrian experiences in various locations around the world, including Morocco, Namibia, Kenya and Northern Ireland. Experiences vary from long-distance explorations, beach walks, jumping lessons and vacations. Here is a short selection:

- **Skeleton Coast:** a ten-night experience in Namibia, exploring the *Skeleton Coast*, with the possibility of long distances to be covered on horseback.
- **Masai Mara Safari:** a seven-night safari in Kenya, through lands loved by Ernest Hemingway and Karen Blixen.
- **The Agadir Sable d'or Ride (Golden Sands of Agadir):** a seven-night experience in Morocco, with long gallops on sandy roads and through deserted villages.
- **Morocco Sand Dune Ride:** a seven-night experience in Morocco, with horseback riding on the edges of the Sahara, from *Ourzazate.*

https://www.equitours.com/

Cavago

An online platform to book equestrian experiences and holidays around the world. **Cavago** promotes the experience of the love and joy of horses, celebrating global horse culture and joining a global community of horse lovers.

https://www.mycavago.com/

Rocking Horse Ranch Resort

It offers various horseback riding adventures, with some guidelines and policies to ensure safety and enjoyment during excursions.

https://www.rockinghorseranch.com/all-inclusive-activities/horse-adventures/

Donkey Experience

Walking and trekking in the company of donkeys.

Donkey Experiences offer a unique adventure, allowing participants to explore nature and connect with donkeys in a special and relaxing way. Although they share some similarities with the **Horse Experiences**, donkey adventures have their own uniqueness, given the different nature of these animals. Activities can range from gentle walks to more challenging treks, and even moments dedicated to simply relaxing and interacting with these friendly and placid creatures.

Donkey Walking Experience

A donkey experience in the peaceful surroundings of the family farm in *Wicklow*.

https://clissmannhorsecaravans.com/donkey-experience/

Zen Donkey Experience

Zen Donkey Experience (ZDx) offers a therapeutic path through interactions with donkeys, also focusing on their rescue. The organization aims to promote the well-being of people and donkeys through experiences in a therapeutic agricultural context, inspired by nature and a plant-based lifestyle. The programs offered aim to enhance quality of life by developing equine-assisted skills, self-empowerment and relationship building, especially through bonding with rescued donkeys.

https://zendonkeyexperience.org/

Animal Experience

Animal Experiences offer an immersion in the world of wildlife, allowing observations and interactions with various animal species in their natural habitat or in protected environments. These experiences can take many forms, each with a specific and unique focus on animal life.

Some subcategories of Animal Experience might include:

- **Birdwatching Experience:** *birdwatching* is an activity that involves the observation and study of birds in nature. This may include listening to their songs, photographing and recording species sighted.
- **Safari Experience:** safaris allow you to get close to wildlife, often in exotic environments such as the African savannah, offering the chance to observe animals such as lions, elephants and giraffes in their natural habitat.
- **Wildlife Sanctuary Visit:** visits to animal sanctuaries or shelters offer an up-close look at the efforts made to protect and conserve animals, often providing a safe haven for species that have been rescued or are endangered.

Maasai Mara National Reserve, Kenya

A protected area offering wildlife viewing safaris, including the annual wildebeest migration.

https://www.maasaimara.com/

The David Sheldrick Wildlife Trust, Kenya

An elephant orphanage that offers the chance to adopt a baby elephant and watch it being fed and bathed in the mud.

https://www.sheldrickwildlifetrust.org/

Marine Life Experience

Experiences that allow you to observe and sometimes interact with marine life, such as whales, dolphins, and other marine creatures.

Some subcategories of Marine Life Experience might include:

- **Whale Watching:** observe whales in their natural environment, often during their seasonal migration.
- **Dolphin Tours:** boat trips or snorkeling with the aim of seeing dolphins in their natural habitat.
- **Scuba Diving or Snorkeling:** scuba diving or snorkeling in areas where you can observe a variety of marine life, such as corals, fish, and sometimes even sharks and turtles.
- **Seal Watching:** observe seals as they rest on cliffs or beaches, or as they swim and play in the water.
- **Turtle Watching:** observe sea turtles, often during nesting season when female turtles come ashore to lay their eggs.

Great Barrier Reef Diving, Australia

Dive or snorkel in the Great Barrier Reef to observe marine life up close.

https://greatbarrierreef.org/

Whale Watching in Kaikoura, New Zealand

Kaikoura is renowned for its whale watching experiences.

https://whalewatch.co.nz/kia-ora/

Marine Life Experience (Palermo)

Guided dives dedicated to learning about the underwater environments of Ustica and the species of flora and fauna that inhabit them.

https://palermodiving.com/it/marine-life-experience

Marine Life Experience (Hawaii)

Experiences of exploration and connection with the marine environment are offered at the **Four Seasons Resort Hualalai**. Whether interest focuses on the island's diverse landforms, Hawaii's unique anchialine ponds, the 60 species of fish housed in *King's Pond*, or local tilapia and oyster farming, the Resort's naturalists create educational experiences destined to remain etched in the memory.

https://www.fourseasons.com/hualalai/services-and-amenities/marine-life-experiences/

Flight Experience

Flight experiences that allow participants to experience flight in various forms and contexts. These experiences offer unique perspectives and panoramic views of the landscape below.

Some of the forms that a **Flight Experience** can take:

- **Paragliding**
- **Hang gliding**
- **Hot air balloon**
- **Helicopter flight**
- **Glider flight**
- **Bungee jumping**
- **Light Aircraft Flight**
- **Zipline**

The latter is an experience that allows individuals to slide along a cable, thanks to the use of a pulley and a safety harness.

Balloon Tour Experience – Cappadocia

The **Balloon Tour Experience** in Cappadocia, Turkey, is one of the most renowned and spectacular hot air balloon flight experiences in the world. The Cappadocia region is famous for its unique lunar landscape, with its rock formations called 'fairy chimneys', underground cities, and rock-hewn churches.

https://www.itinerariesperienziali.it/en/directory-offerte/listing/balloon-tour-experience-cappadocia/

Sky Combat Ace

It offers an extreme and adventurous flying experience, allowing participants to fly in an Extra 330, with the ability to customize the experience based on their comfort level. Pilots are highly trained and certified by the Federal Aviation Administration (FAA).

https://www.skycombatace.com/

Virgin Experience Gifts

It offers a variety of flight experiences, with options ranging from aerobatic flights to combat flights. Experiences are available at various locations and may include flights in historic or modern aircraft.

https://www.virginexperiencegifts.com/flying

Fishing Tourism Experience

Fishing tourism represents a form of tourism that allows participants to set sail aboard authentic fishing boats, taking part in or simply observing the daily fishing operations alongside local fishermen. Fishing tourism facilitates an intimate connection with the existence and culture of fishing communities, offering an authentic and often compelling adventure. In Italy the fishing tourism activity is regulated by the Legislative Decree of 9 January 2012, art. 2.

Experience Fishing

Experience Fishing is a project led by the Northern Ontario industry that provides participating operators with the essential tools and resources to offer a unique fishing experience, within their activities, to non-fishermen visitors who approach for the first time to this experience.

https://destinationnorthernontario.ca/experience-fishing/

Great Fishing Adventures of Australia

Great Fishing Adventures of Australia represents a collection of leading independent fishing tourism operators who have decided to join forces to jointly raise Australia's profile as an international fishing destination.

https://www.tourism.australia.com/en/resources/industry-resources/industry-programs/signature-experiences-of-australia/great-fishing-adventures-of-australia.html

3.5 Wellness Experience (WLE)

These experiences are related to psycho-physical well-being. It is appropriate to consider the cases in which the **Wellness Experience** is primary from the cases in which it is secondary to other types of experiences. We could therefore make the following distinctions:

- **Primary Wellness Experience:** the experience of well-being is the prevailing aspect of the offer (this is the case, for example, of some SPAs, thermal centers and body care services).
- **Secondary Wellness Experience:** the Wellness Experience is included in other forms of experiences considered prevalent (Guest Experience, Open-Air Experience, Sport Experience, Dinner Experience, etc.)

By using the definition **Secondary Wellness Experiences**, I refer to the individual chapters where I discuss this type of experience.

Wellness Travel And Tours – G Adventures

Platform of tourism offers focused on well-being by G Adventures.

https://www.gadventures.com/travel-styles/wellness/

Plaza Sensory Pool – Sensory pool – Abano Terme

This structure, in addition to being an example of experiential principles (multisensorial, aesthetic approach, immersion, and others) is a classic example of application of the thematic approach.

https://www.itinerariesperienziali.it/en/directory-offerte/listing/plaza-sensory-poll-piscina-sensoriale/

World Spa NYC

Authentic *banyas*, Finnish saunas, Turkish and Moroccan hammams, infrared room, *Clay & Hay* sauna and other experiences can be explored, all crafted at World Spa, which presents a contemporary take on traditional and ancient wellness practices. For a distinctive treatment, access to the eye-catchingly designed salt room offers purification through Himalayan salt therapy, recognized to treat mild respiratory ailments and provide added softness to the skin.

https://www.itinerariesperienziali.it/en/directory-offerte/listing/world-spa-nyc/

3.6 Entertainment and Show Experience (ESE)

These are experiences whose primary offer consists of entertainment activities and shows.

The **Entertainment and Show Experience (ESE)** constitutes a wide range of tourism and leisure experiences, with a main focus on various forms of entertainment and entertainment. Such experiences can include live events, such as concerts, theater plays and artistic performances, but also more established and stable attractions, such as theme parks and family entertainment centers.

Experience The Best Entertainment in USA

A website describing a wide range of entertainment experiences in different locations across the United States.

https://www.visittheusa.com/USAExperiences/entertainment

AVATAR: The Experience Attraction Tour – Singapore

A tour inspired by the magnificence and unique narrative of the highest-grossing film in cinematic history, **Avatar**.

Located in the Cloud Forest, characterized by its iconic view of waterfalls, spiral walkways and a unique architectural glass greenhouse, Avatar: The Experience entices visitors to connect with the extraterrestrial world of Pandora, its bioluminescent environments, mystical creatures , flora and the fascinating culture of its indigenous inhabitants, the *Na'vi*.

https://www.itinerariesperienziali.it/en/directory-offerte/listing/avatar-the-experience-attraction-tour/

Apollo Club – Milan

A cocktail bar, bistro & club in the heart of Milan's Navigli. Reference point for the world of art, music and fashion.

https://www.itinerariesperienziali.it/en/directory-offerte/listing/apollo-club-milano/

3.7 Sports Experience (SPE)

Experiences focused on physical and sporting activity, in which participants are directly involved in events and activities related to the sport in question. In some cases, **Sport Experiences** can also include participation in exclusive sporting events, both local and international.

Sport Experiences are often in close correlation with other categories of experiences, especially with the Open-Air Experience, in particular for those sports in direct contact with nature.

Some possible subcategories of Sport Experiences:

- **Active Participation Experiences:** experiences that directly involve participants in sporting activities, such as surfing courses, mountain bike excursions, or climbing lessons.
- **Spectator Experiences:** experiences that indirectly involve participants who are spectators of sporting events, however, unique and with a strong emotional impact.
- **Learning and Training Experiences:** experiences that offer training and learning in a specific sport.
- **Adventure Sports Experiences:** experiences involving adventure and adrenaline-filled sports, such as skydiving, rafting, or scuba diving.

Mont Blanc Ultra-Trail

An extremely challenging and scenic ultramarathon, covering 106 miles and taking runners over more than 30.000 feet of elevation gain across three countries: France, Switzerland and Italy, all set during a weekly late summer party in the Alpine town of Chamonix.

https://www.gq.com/story/18-best-live-sports-events

Sailing Experience

In places such as Tuscany, around the Island of Elba, in the Bay of Genoa, in Portofino, in Naples, in Sardinia or along the enchanting scenery of the Cinque Terre, there are isolated beaches and hidden coves of unparalleled beauty. All Sport coordinates sailing regattas for groups of six participants on beautifully designed boats, offering an experience focused on competition and team collaboration.

https://www.allsport.it/vela

GT Driving Experience

All Sport offers the opportunity to experience the thrill of a lap on the track aboard a Ferrari or Lamborghini in the main Italian circuits: Monza, Imola, Mugello, Varano de Melegari, Tazio Nuvolari (PV), Franciacorta (BS) and Vallelunga (RM).

During the experience, guests are always accompanied by a CSAI-licensed professional driver, who provides instructions on the fundamental techniques for correct track driving, allowing you to savor the uniqueness of the moment in complete safety.

https://www.allsport.it/drivingexperience

Rome Sport Experience

https://youtu.be/9N5vGn2-lCw?si=tXZbAdGxp0QrwY-5

3.8 Experiential Marketing (EMA)

Experiential Marketing: when the experience is instrumental to the provision of services or sale of products. This approach goes beyond traditional advertising and often takes the form of creating events aimed at establishing emotional bonds between the brand and the consumer through engaging and unforgettable experiences.

In the chapter titled 'From Product to Experiences' I have already indicated some examples of Experiential Marketing, I won't dwell on it and refer to the **Experiences Database** for further examples.

https://www.itinerariesperienziali.it/en/banche-dati-offerte-esperienziali/

4. Experiential Quality

4.1 The Concept of Quality

Definition of Quality:

The origin of wisdom is the definition of terms.
(Socrates)

ISO 9000:2005 (Fundamentals and Vocabulary) provides the following definition:

Quality: Ability of a set of characteristics inherent in a product, system, or process to meet the requirements of customers and other interested parties.

The following definition has then been revised with the new revision of UNI EN ISO 9000:2015.

Quality: Degree to which a set of intrinsic characteristics of an object satisfies the requirements.

This last definition, instead, comes closest to the definition I have been using since 2013:

Quality: Capability of a set of characteristics, pertinent to an **entity**, to confirm the expectations referable to it by all the **interested parties**.

Therefore, there is the need to identify, for each area, the elements at the basis of the concept of quality:

- **the entity to which the quality is to be applied**: a specific product, system, service, activity, organization or any of the previous combinations (in our case we could also talk about experiential paths, interpretation paths, installations, interpretation services, etc.)
- **expectations (needs)**: this is what the interested parties expect, in the case of experiences and interpretation paths, by simplifying and narrowing the circle, we can think of the participants in the experiential path and the ways in which this is offered.
- **interested parties (those who express expectations or needs) according to the entity**: which, depending on the case, can be called customer, user, tourist, user of the cultural good or service, student, guest, participant, citizen, authority or even the community itself.

We reinforce the definition just given by stating that quality also equals the ability to achieve the established objectives (effectiveness), but we shouldn't forget to do it in the best possible way; in fact, when available human, material and financial resources are scarce, it is vitally important to optimize what one has available (**efficiency**).

Speaking of interested parties, we must not forget that we often refer to cultural heritage, and therefore to the cultural heritage that belongs to the entire country; in reality, an in-depth analysis should make us understand that the subjects interested in cultural heritage are not only us, but also posterity. I have already had the opportunity to write in this regard that we can talk about promoting and reevaluating *our* cultural heritage, we can affirm our right to take advantage of the immense cultural heritage (tangible and immaterial) that surrounds us, but this should never make us forget the duty to keep it intact for posterity.

In the early nineties, when I began my journey of promoting Sicilian cultural heritage, I had the opportunity to say: «While respecting the present, we must be on the side of the future, as we will be whatever it will find. »

Expectations (needs)

This is what interested parties expect.

Expectations (needs) can be:

- explicit,
- implied
- mandatory

Explicit expectations

The simplest to identify is the following: if the experiential offer has been communicated correctly and exhaustively, this is what the user will explain when making a booking:

- the request for a reservation of an offer can be explicitly indicated in documentary form in the form of an order, possibly online, but where it is admissible, also verbally.
- the request for a health service (e.g. analysis) can be explicitly indicated in documentary form in the medical prescription, but where it is admissible, also verbally.
- the request for a margherita pizza in a pizzeria is explicit by the customer.
- The request to design an educational path based on contents and objectives explicitly indicated by the client is explicit.

Implied expectations

Implicit expectations are those that are unlikely to be made explicit even if they form the basis of the offer itself.

The participant in an experiential journey will probably not explicitly declare them, but depending on the type of event, some of the following aspects may be part of his expectations:

- a memorable experience
- courtesy
- welcome
- compliance with the contents of the promised service
- compliance with the established deadlines
- difficulties of the activities constituting the experience that are compatible with one's psycho-physical abilities
- acquire new knowledge
- discover new aspects of life and the territory
- involvement
- evasion
- aesthetic needs (aesthetics and self-realization[9])
- When requesting a health service which involves, for example, blood sampling, it is implicit that this occurs without pain or unpleasant consequences.
- When requesting a hotel reservation, the room cleaning service is generally implied.
- When requesting a *pizza margherita*, it is usually implied that it is not burnt.

Mandatory expectations

We are here referring to compliance with rules and laws in force, or other technical standards possibly unknown to the user of the service:

- privacy legislation
- safety legislation
- food hygiene regulations (HACCP)
- rights of the tourist

---

[9] A proposito del bisogno di autorealizzazione si veda la scala dei bisogni di Abraham H. Maslow

- regulations on the information to be provided for the products or services used to support the service offered
- etc.

For example:

- The request for a tourist service implies compliance with rules and laws such as compliance with the privacy law or other rules, possibly not known to the customer/user/participant/guest.
- The preparation of the pizza requested by the customer implies compliance with standards such as food safety (HACCP) or the use of products permitted by law.
- That the equipment made available and the methods of use of the hiking route comply with the required safety regulations.

The Factors of Quality

Once **quality** has been defined, it is necessary to **measure** it, but to do this it is necessary to equip oneself with an appropriate quality measurement system.

Of course, a system for measuring quality in the areas that are of interest to us, which is effective and compliant with operational reality, will have to consider several factors that will have to be systematically identified.

Therefore, in addition to the **entity,** to which the concept of quality is applied, and the interested parties (who expresses expectations or needs according to the entity, there is also the need to identify **quality factors**.

Quality factors will have to then be transformed into measurable indicators, to be able to make comparisons. It is through the application of these factors that the expectations of the various interested parties are confirmed.

A system for measuring quality in the experiential sector will have to take into account several factors, some strictly dependent on the type of activity, others common to multiple types of activity.

In some cases, instead of *factors*, the term *size* is used.

A few years ago, in my work[10] , inspired by the quality factors proposed by Zeithamal, Parassuraman and Berry (1991), integrated with some factors recommended by the CiVIT 88/2010 and 3/2012 guidelines and by others hypothesized by me, I proposed a classification of quality factors and indicators. In the same work I also proposed the model (called the **Six Steps Technique**) for the identification of factors and quality indicators that was well suited to tourist services.

---

[10] Ignazio Caloggero - Qualità, Modelli Operativi e Competitività dell'Offerta Turistica. ISBN: 9788894321906 - 2017

The Six Step Technique[11]

- First step: Identification of the Entities involved
- Second step: Identification of interested parties
- Third step: Identification of processes (Process Map)
- Fourth step: identification of quality factors (dimensions)
- Fifth step: transition from factors to quality indicators
- Sixth step: Identification of quality standards

I translated the results of the study at the time into a series of articles and in-depth reports, within the project "Quality in the Tourism, Artistic and Entertainment Sector - Tourism, Arts and Entertainment Quality Improvement (TAEQI)". This project is available to the community to the address indicated below and to which I refer for details, since here I will limit myself to dealing only with the elements of particular interest for the experiential aspects.

Link to the TAEQI project:

https://www.aiptoc.it/tourism-art-and-entertainment-quality-improvement-taeqi/

[11] La tecnica dei sei passi prende spunto dalla delibera CiVIT n. 88/2010 e da alcuni principi indicati dallo schema generale di riferimento della carta dei servizi pubblici sanitari (D.P.C.M. 19 maggio 1995). Ho adattato la metodologia proposta al caso delle offerte culturali e dei servizi turistici in genere.

One of the steps that is necessary for the identification of factors and indicators is the so-called 'process mapping'. This phase essentially corresponds to identifying and defining the highlights of the flow of activities (and therefore of the services provided) which affect the overall quality of the experiential/interpretative path.

To describe these moments, the phrase 'moments of the user experience' is often used. The meaning given to the word *experience*, in these cases, is much broader than the **concept** of experience, which is instead attributed when talking about experiential paths: in this case, it is not a question of identifying only the *experiential* moments, but **all** the moments, and therefore the related processes that involve the participants, since, even if apparently not linked to the direct use by the participant, they can affect the final service (experience).

This is achieved by retracing the user's **experience** (in its broadest sense) and analyzing all the moments of his stay in the place (and the structures involved), or of his contact with the providers of the experiential/interpretive path.

Without going into the details of the six-step technique (in-depth information in the link previously provided), I leave a list below illustrative and not exhaustive of particularly significant Quality Factors, linked to an experiential/interpretive path[12] :

FB Base Factors

Technical quality

- FB2: Expertise
- FB7: Reliability
- FB12: Security
- FB13: Infrastructure and Equipment

Relational quality

- FB1: Courtesy
- FB3: Empathy

[12] Per l'elenco aggiornato e la descrizione dei singoli fattori rimando al link fornito

- FB5: Reception
- FB6: Communication

Organizational quality

- FB4: Flexibility
- FB8: Transparency
- FB9: Timeliness
- FB10: Continuity
- FB11: Elasticity
- FB16: General accessibility (websites, presence of communication tools (timetables, distance, transport, etc.)

Social quality

- FB14: Protection
- FB15: Motivation

FA Equity/Accessibility Factors based on needs

- FA1: Motor accessibility
- FA2: Visual accessibility
- FA3: Hearing accessibility
- FA4: Social accessibility
- FA5: Economic accessibility
- FA6: Food accessibility
- FA7: Environmental accessibility
- FA8: Accessibility for pets
- FA9: Accessibility for family members (children, elderly)
- FA10: Accessibility for additional special needs (e.g. mental or psychic disabilities)

FS: Sustainability Factors

- FS1: Energy Sustainability
- FS2: Food Sustainability
- FS3: Sustainability of Mobility
- FS4: Sustainability of Communications
- FS5: Sustainability of Packaging
- FS6: Sustainability of Waste
- FS7: Sustainability of Suppliers
- FS8: Sustainability of locations for events and meetings
- FS9: Management Sustainability

FC: Context Factors (Context, attractions and local resources)

- FC1: Health and Hygiene (sanitary conditions, epidemics)
- FC2: Public Safety (crime, violence, terrorism phenomena)
- FC3; Pricing Policy
- FC4: Sustainability Policies
- FC5: Development Policies and Incentives
- FC6: Innovation
- FC7: Participatory Policies
- FC8: Endogenous Attractions
- FC9: Induced Attractions
- FC10: Hardware Resources
- FC11: Software Resources

A clarification on the last four factors (FC8, FC9, FC10 and FC11).

Attractions and resources

The **Tourist Heritage**, which is the basis of the cultural or tourist offer, includes all those elements, that can constitute a tourist interest (attractions), and is the union of the following elements:

- **Cultural heritage** in the broadest sense of the term: tangible (historical-artistic, natural, archaeological) and immaterial (food and wine, demo-ethno-anthropological heritage, traditions, history, culture) capable of promoting touristic interest.
- **Unconventional tourist attractions**: Other elements of potential tourist interest may be certain conditions or elements, such as the climate or the morphology of the territory, or induced attractions (structures/activities created specifically by man: tourist infrastructures, shows, special events, recreational and sporting activities, etc.)

The attractions can also be divided into:

- **Endogenous attractions:** natural attractions (mountains, lakes, beaches, rivers, climate, etc.) or cultural attractions (cooking, crafts, language, customs, monuments, historical facts, etc.).
- **Induced attractions:** tourist infrastructures, special events, recreational and sporting activities, etc.

Resources: Services (tourist and auxiliary), structures and infrastructures that assume the function of facilitating the use of the attractions, in turn divided into:

- **Hardware resources:** Infrastructures, structures and tools used for the provision of tourist and non-tourist services.
- **Software resources:** Purely tourist services (reception, catering, entertainment, transport, information offices, etc.), auxiliary services that favor the accessibility and usability of attractions, financial resources (including loans and incentives).

I used the term **Quality Factors**; in recent years, as already written, we talk about dimensional evaluation of quality using the term *Dimensions of Quality*, however giving different definitions and identifying several different dimensions depending on the reality or of the model to which the multidimensional evaluation principle has been applied.

Quality Indicators

Quality factors are the main tool for the perception of quality by those who express needs/expectations.

The quality indicators, on the other hand, are quantitative (and therefore measurable) variables that make it possible to measure the quality level as a whole, as they are considered *indicative* of the quality factor, they are therefore objective indicators and can be:

- **System indicators:** include structural, technological and organizational indicators.
- **Result indicators:** indicators relating to direct measurements by users relating to perceived quality (service user satisfaction indicators) or by specialized personnel (external evaluators, mystery auditors).
- **Process indicators:** include the presence of specific operational procedures and processes.
- **Context indicators:** include external indicators that are not always directly controllable by the direct managers of the tourist offer (public transport, roads, taxis, external signage, tourist information, etc.)

Here is a brief non-exhaustive example of indicators of a general nature:

System indicators

Management (main factors affected: Reliability, Expertise, Safety, Accessibility/Equity)

- Presence of a Safety Management System
- Presence of an Event Sustainability Management System

- Presence of a Management System for Experiential Offers

Information (main factors involved: Communication, Reliability, Expertise, Security, Accessibility, Reception)

- Active website
- Presence on the main social media platforms (Facebook, Instagram, X, etc.)
- Accessible website (e-accessibility, W3C, Law 4/2004, etc.)
- Multilingual website presence
- Presence of a contact form and information on the services provided on the website
- Presence of useful information on the website for identifying the meeting or starting point for the scheduled visit (possibly on an interactive map - Google Maps)
- Presence of the minimum information provided when communicating the offer
- Presence of information to be given to the participant during the purchase phase
- Presence of information to be given to the participant during the experience
- Presence of information points near and inside the place object of the experience

Barriers (motor, visual, auditory and economic needs) (main factors affected: accessibility).

Indicators related to motor needs

Indicators associated with any support or refreshment facilities (information points, catering, accommodation, leisure centers, (eco)museum facilities, environmental education centers, huts, etc.):

- Easy path to access the structure (minimum width of 90 cm and spaces for reversing)
- Doors and entrance passages accessible independently with wheelchairs (net opening of at least 80 cm)

- Doors and passageways in internal areas accessible independently with wheelchairs (clear opening of at least 75 cm and height differences not exceeding 2,5 cm)
- Presence of toilets for the disabled (access dimensional parameters, maneuvering spaces, arrangement of sanitary appliances in accordance with the law)
- Presence of lifts for disabled people (dimensional access parameters, maneuvering spaces, control layout compliant with regulations).

Indicators associated with the mobility of the itinerary (in case of field experiences)

- Absence of elements that make the route difficult: stony, with gravel, sand, grass, mud, etc.)
- Absence of obstacles: holes, vegetation, stones, steps, bridges, low walls, etc.)
- Not too steep slope (from 7 to 12%)
- Presence of benches
- Presence of benches equipped with armrests on the sides
- Presence of handrails along the path
- Width of the path or access gates suitable for wheelchairs

Indicators related to sensory needs (sight)

- Presence of signs and tactile maps
- Presence of information in braille
- Presence of audio guides

Indicators related to sensory needs (hearing)

- Video guides with writing or LIS
- Presence of adequate visual signs
- Presence of experienced LIS personnel

Result indicators (main factors affected: all)

- Clarity in displaying services when booking/purchasing
- Staff able to treat users in a kind and courteous way
- Infrastructure (absence of well-functioning plants, vehicles or support structures)
- Equipment (absence of tools and non-functioning equipment)
- Absence of physical risks except those reasonably foreseen for areas associated with guided tours and correct management of the latter
- Absence of activities and behaviors in violation of the principles of sustainability
- Ability to respect times (compliance with the timetable, from departure to arrival)
- Absence of unexpected program changes not dictated by the needs of the case (emergencies, unforeseen obstacles, etc.)
- Waiting times for ticket purchase (accessibility)
- Presence of competent personnel
- Presence of courteous staff

Appearance of the premises (any support or refreshment premises):

- No risk
- Absence of dirt
- Presence of the minimum equipment required for the type of structure

Context indicators (main factors affected: accessibility)

- Presence of adequate and safe roads to reach the pre-established meeting point/s or the assets to be visited
- Presence of public/private transport to reach the pre-established meeting point(s) (number and location) or the assets to be visited
- Presence of public parking near the pre-established meeting point(s) or the assets to be visited (number and location, free parking, average times to find parking)

- Accessibility to monuments and points of interest (opening hours adapted to tourist demand)
- Presence of clear and adequate signage which facilitates access to monuments and points of interest.

It should be underlined that some factors are closely correlated with each other; for example, many of the indicators linked to the **communication factor** favor the **accessibility factor** itself. The presence of a website, in addition to being an indicator for the communication factor, is also a tool that facilitates knowledge of the asset, and therefore also accessibility.

Quality Standards

Let's take a look at further definitions:

- **Quality standards.** Expected value for a certain indicator. They can be divided into general standards and specific standards.
- **General quality standards**. They represent quality objectives that refer to the overall performance provided and are generally expressed by statistical average values of the indicators (e.g. percentages of complaints compared to the number of customers in the year less than 1%).
- **Specific quality standards**. They represent quality objectives that refer to each of the individual services provided to the user, who can directly verify compliance, and are generally expressed by a maximum or minimum threshold relating to the values that the indicator can take on. (maximum waiting time at the restaurant of the reservation within 15 minutes).

Here are some examples of quality standards:

Information search. Quality standards

- Telephone number to receive information active from 9:00 to 18:00
- Accessible type website (e-accessibility, W3C,)
- Multilingual website (Italian, English, French and Spanish)
- Multilingual staff (Italian, English, French and Spanish) available for information

Acceptance of Quality Standards

- Multilingual staff (Italian, English, French and Spanish) available at check-in
- Parking spaces for the disabled adequately marked near the entrances
- Easy path to access the structure (minimum width of 90 cm and spaces for reversing)

- Doors and entrance passages accessible independently with wheelchairs (net opening of at least 80 cm)
- Presence of signs and tactile maps (sight)
- Presence of information in braille (view)
- Presence of adequate visual signs (hearing)
- Opening of the Castle from 9.00 to 00
- Opening of the Castle 7 days a week
- Maximum wait to buy the ticket 20 min.

As you can easily see, the standards can be different from structure to structure, depending on their own policies that aim to provide a realistic service linked to their available resources.

Quality standards should however be placed in a context of continuous improvement of the quality provided, so they should be monitored and improved over time (quality objectives).

4.3 Factors and Indicators of Experiential Quality

At this point, we must integrate the previous factors with the following ones, which do nothing other than fully reflect the experiential principles.

Experiential Quality Factors

Experiential Factors (EF)

- FE1: Multisensory Approach
- FE2: Cultural approach
- FE3: Uniqueness
- FE4: Relational approach
- FE5: Direct participation
- FE6: Experiential learning
- FE7: Thematic approach
- FE8: Aesthetic approach
- FE9: Entertainment
- FE10: Immersion

I refer you to the chapter relating to experiential principles, which in some cases also presents real examples, making the indicators that allow you to respect the 10 factors just listed quite clear.

Below is just a summary of what has already been stated.

Experiential indicators

FE1 Factor: Multisensory Approach

Indicators:

- Presence of activities that involve most of the senses: sight, hearing, touch, smell and in some cases, taste
- Use of multimedia technology or other measures capable of stimulating multiple senses including the senses of smell, hearing and touch
- Use of sensory marketing techniques

Factor FE2: Cultural approach (Local identities)

Indicators:

- Presence of activities that involve the knowledge or understanding of cultural, natural, historical or demo-ethno-anthropological elements of the place

Factor FE3: Uniqueness

Indicators:

- The uniqueness of the cultural experience or interpretation, both being linked to local identities and specific places, lies precisely in its nature. However, it is advisable to avoid that the experience/interpretation paths are associated with either purely serial or mass offers, which would in some way diminish their uniqueness.

Factor FE4: Relational approach

Indicators:

- Relationship-based experiential/interpretive offering
- Use of empathetic communication oriented towards the centrality of the participant

The indicators reported are part of what we have called 'result indicators', as they can be detected directly by the participants or by specialized personnel (external evaluators, mystery auditors).

Factor FE5: Direct participation

Indicators:

- Presence of activities that see the direct and active participation of the participants
- Presence of methodologies and technologies that encourage interactivity on the part of the participants

Factor FE6: Experiential learning

Indicators:

- Presence of experiential learning activities

Factor FE7: Thematic approach

Indicators:

- An experiential journey characterized by a theme that characterizes it and which constitutes its common thread.

Factor FE8: Aesthetic approach

Indicators:

- Presence of scenic elements and reference context that favor the aesthetic aspect: atmosphere, respect for the concept of beauty, place chosen for the experience, plot (script) consistent with the chosen theme and the identified place.

Factor FE9: Entertainment

Indicators:

- Presence of moments of entertainment that enrich, 'lighten' and make the experience pleasant.

Factor FE10: Immersion

Indicators:

- Presence of immersive techniques and respect for the principles of direct participation and aesthetic approach.

4.4 Evaluation of the Quality of the Experiential Offers

The final quality of the experiential path is not only linked to the quality factors, but must also take into account other moments, which concern for example the very context of the organization offering the experience, as well as other activities such as: planning, designing, 'staging' the experiences, and evaluation and improvement activities. Essentially, we could say that the quality of an experiential offer is not superior to the quality of the organization that provides it.

Therefore, organizations that provide experiential offers, in order to monitor and maintain a high level of quality of their offers, should adapt their organizational system by implementing a real **Management System of Experiential Offers** (SGOE) which takes into account the type of offers provided.

In this perspective, I have developed a **Proposal for a Technical Standard for the Management System of Experiential Offers** (SGOE), currently called SGOE-01. This was developed taking inspiration from the **High Level Structure** (HLS), adopted for several years in all ISO standards relating to the certification of Management Systems. HLS (or SAL, in the Italian version) was designed to serve as a common foundation for all other standards, thus facilitating compatibility and integration with other certification schemes (Annex SL of the ISO Directives – Part I). The objective of adopting the HLS structure is to ensure a homogeneous application of basic texts, terms and definitions.

On the basis of some requirements indicated by the proposed technical standard SGOE-CSH01, the VQE (Experiential Quality Evaluation) evaluation scheme was created, based, in version 2.5, on the measurement of 40 indicators divided into main areas and several sub-areas.

In brackets we can find the number of requirements:

- CO: Context of the Organization and Leadership (4)
- PI: Planning (5)
- UP: Support (5)

- OA: Operational Activities (20)
  - QT: Technical quality (2)
  - QR: Relational quality (3)
  - QO: Organizational quality (1)
  - FE: Experiential Quality (10)
  - MS: Staging (3)
  - FO: Control of externally supplied services and products (1)
- VM: Evaluation and Continuous Improvement (6)

Note:

- The term **experiential path** is synonymous with **experiential event**
- For each factor, the necessary measures for its measurement and evaluation should also be implemented.

The VQE self-assessment methodology is made available to all organizations that wish to measure their organizational capacity in the provision of experiential offers. The VQE methodology can be used by an organization for:

- **Self-evaluation**: as a self-assessment tool for measuring the quality of one's experiential offerings
- **Customer satisfaction increase**: as a tool to increase the satisfaction of its customers through the effective application of the principles of experiential quality to its experientials
- **Obtaining the Experiential Quality Mark**: as a tool that demonstrates compliance with the requirements necessary for obtaining the Experiential Quality Mark ®

Each organization can freely decide which indicators to adopt. For organizations that wish to obtain the **Experiential Quality Mark**, which certifies their organizational capacity to provide quality experiential offers, the mandatory indicators are indicated (O) and recommended (R).

Some requirements may not apply (NA) to the operational reality of some organizations. In these cases, these requirements do not need to be implemented and will have no impact on the final score.

The recommended requirements, although not individually mandatory, must be taken into consideration, as the Quality Mark can only be obtained if at least 70% of the applicable and recommended requirements are met.

The version and updated list of indicators can be seen at the following web address:

https://www.itinerariesperienziali.it/en/la-metodologia-vqe-per-la-valutazione-della-qualita-delle-offerte-esperienziali-di-una-organizzazione/

VQE requirements

CONTEXT OF THE ORGANIZATION

Understanding of the organization and its context

- CO1 (R): Has the Organization determined external and internal factors relevant to its purpose that could impact its ability to achieve the intended objectives of its experiential events?
- CO2 (R) Is information regarding these factors periodically monitored and reviewed?

Understanding the needs and expectations of interested parties

- CO3: (R) Has the organization determined the needs and expectations of these interested parties?

Note: *needs* can be explicit, implicit and mandatory

Roles and responsibilities and authorities

- CO4: (R) Has the organization defined and communicated responsibilities and authorities for relevant roles within the organization (e.g. organizational chart and job description)?

PLANNING

Has the organization planned the activities necessary for the correct execution of the experiential events?

Does activity planning cover at least the following aspects?

- PI1 (O) The processes necessary for the realization of the experience

- PI2 (O) The human resources necessary for the implementation of the activities (possibly with the relative organizational chart and job description where the hierarchies, tasks and responsibilities are defined)?
- PI3 (O) Permits, licenses and necessary authorizations
- PI4 (O) The equipment and infrastructure necessary for the activities. Particularly in terms of:
    - o buildings and related systems
    - o Equipment and related maintenance
- PI5 (R) The entities involved (public and private entities involved in the preparation and implementation of the activities).

SUPPORT

Human resources

- SU1 (O) Has the organization determined the knowledge required for the operation of its processes?
- SU2 (R) Does the Events Manager have a professional certification pursuant to law 4/2013?
- SU3 (R) Does the organization take actions to acquire the necessary skills or to maintain them? (e.g. training programs)

Communication

- SU4 (R) Has the organization determined the internal communications necessary for the correct performance of activities?
- SU5 (R) Has the organization determined the necessary tools for correct external communication?

OPERATING ACTIVITIES

Quality Factors

Has the Organization determined the factors and related quality indicators applicable to its operational processes? Please answer for each individual factor indicated. For each factor, the necessary measures for its measurement and evaluation must also be adopted.

Technical quality factors

- QT1 (O) FB12: Safety: absence of dangers for the public, compliance with safety regulations
- QT2 (O) FB13: Infrastructure and Equipment: quality of infrastructure, materials, equipment and tools

Relational quality factors

- QR1(R) FB1 Courtesy: kindness, respect, consideration and cordiality of the staff towards the users
- QR2(R) FB5 Reception: pleasant, welcoming and comfortable environments, pleasant appearance of the structures, equipment and staff, additional courtesy services
- QR3(R) FB6 Communication: availability and ability to listen to interested parties, complete information relating to the services provided, use of understandable language

Organizational Quality Factors

- QO1(R) FB16 General accessibility: Ability to make the proposed activities accessible linked to multiple aspects (adequate opening hours, parking, information on opening hours, transport, etc.) and also to the ease of contact and compliance.

Experiential Quality Factors

- FE1: **Multisensory Approach**: does the experiential path include multisensory activities (involvement of the senses: sight, hearing, touch, smell and, where possible, taste)?
- FE2: **Cultural Approach**: does the experiential path allow you to deepen your knowledge of elements of local identity?
- FE3: **Uniqueness**: does the experiential path have unique characteristics?
- FE4: **Relational approach**: is the experiential path based on human relationships?
- FE5: **Direct participation**: does the experiential path involve the direct participation of the guest in some activities?
- FE6: **Experiential learning**: does the experiential path include a learning phase through the direct participation of the guest in some activities?
- FE7: **Thematic approach**: each experiential path is built starting from a theme that characterizes it and which constitutes its common thread.
- FE8: **Aesthetic approach**: the aesthetic approach is one of the elements, together with that of direct participation, at the basis of the concept of *immersion*. The events that constitute 'the staging of the experience' must be designed in such a way as to give importance to all aspects that can influence aesthetics: the atmosphere, the sense of beauty, the place chosen for the experience, the plot (screenplay) which must be consistent with the chosen theme and the identified location.
- FE9: **Entertainment**: the experiential path should also include moments of entertainment that enrich and make the experience pleasant.
- FE10: **Immersion**: the principle of immersion is the actual direct consequence of the application of the principles of multisensory, direct participation and aesthetic approach.

Whether the Experiential Quality Factors are obligatory or not is linked to the possible request for the Brand.

The Experiential Quality Seal (QE) is applied to the following experiences:

- Authentic Experience: (application of the following requirements: FE1, FE3, FE4, FE5, FE7)
- Authentic Cultural Experience: (application of the following requirements: FE1, FE2, FE3, FE4, FE5, FE6, and FE7)

The Experiential Quality Seal of Excellence is applied to the following experiences:

- Full Experience (of Excellence): (application of the following requirements: FE1, FE3, FE4, FE5, FE7, FE8, FE9, FE10)
- Full Cultural Experience (of Excellence): (application of the following requirements: FE1, FE2, FE3, FE4, FE5, FE6, FE7, FE8, FE9, FE10

Elements of staging

- MS1 (R) Has the organization inserted appropriate positive clues (stimuli) that harmonize impressions?
- MS2 (R) Has the organization eliminated any negative clues that distract from the theme or aesthetic context?
- MS3 (R) Has the organization integrated the experience with mementos (souvenirs)?

Control services and products supplied from outside

- FO1 (R) Where experiences include outsourced products/services, has the organization implemented procedures for the necessary controls so that they do not negatively affect the objectives set for the same experiences?

EVALUATION AND IMPROVEMENT

Monitoring and evaluation

Has the Organization determined a set of quality factors and indicators that will be monitored and evaluated? Do these factors include at least the following factors?

- VM1 Technical quality
- VM2 Relational quality
- VM3 Experiential quality? (FE1-FE10)
- VM4 Has the organization implemented a system to control perceived quality? (Customer satisfaction)
- VM5 Does the organization conduct internal audits at planned intervals?
- VM6 Has the organization implemented a system for managing nonconformities and corrective actions?

4.5. Experiential Quality Seal ®

The transition from an economy of service to an economy of the experience is clear for all to see; the transformation now concerns not only the area that are historically linked to tourism, but also those of services and product marketing (experiential marketing). This entails the need to distinguish experiential offers from a simple offer that only bears the label of experiential. This is important not only for the host of experiences (tourist or simple user of an experiential event) who must choose among the countless offers present in the area, but also for tourist and cultural operators who intend to offer memorable events that involve individuals on the personal plan. Customers who ask for products and services are now replaced by "guests" looking for emotions to remember, and if these emotions are attested through a **Quality Mark**, that is even better.

The Quality Mark guarantees compliance with experiential and organizational Quality requirements; it does so through a formal certificate issued to organizations that provide experiential offers, following a careful evaluation of objective evidence and in compliance with the principle of impartiality and according to an international standard.

Experiential Activities for which organizations can obtain the Quality Seal: all activities indicated in the Repertoire of Experiential Activities to which I refer you for further details.

The requirements are measured through the checklist which reports the indicators provided by the VQE Standard evaluation of experiential quality seen in the previous chapter.

For detailed information on the Experiential Quality Mark, please refer to the dedicated web area:

https://www.centrostudihelios.it/il-marchio-di-qualita-esperienziale-qe/

5. The Experiential Professions

5.1 The recognition of Experience Professionals in Italy

In Italy there is a path for the legitimation of experience professionals, as well as for other figures linked to the tourism area. Currently, considering that this profession is not regulated, it is governed by Law 4/2013. Furthermore, a decree was recently published which, for the first time, provides an official definition of 'professional'.

The Prime Ministerial Decree of 14/10/2021, known as the **Recruitment Decree** and published in the Official Journal no. 268 of 10/11/2021, provides for the first time a legal definition of *professional.* This decree identifies the professionals who are authorized to submit applications on the recruitment portal to obtain professional positions in public administrations.

For the purposes of the decree, the word *professional* means the following: *the natural person registered in a professional register, college or association and professionals as defined pursuant to art. 1 of law 14 January 2013, n. 4, in possession of the certification of quality and professional qualification of the services pursuant to art. 7 of law 14 January 2013, n. 4, issued by a professional association included in the list of the Ministry of Economic Development, or in possession of certification in compliance with the UNI technical standard pursuant to art. 9 of law 14 January 2013, n. 4 (Art. 1 Prime Ministerial Decree 14/10/2021).*

In summary, according to the Prime Ministerial Decree of 14/10/2021, the recognized professionals are:

- Professionals registered in a professional register, college or association.
- Professionals who hold a Quality and Professional Qualification certificate, issued according to Law 4/2013.
- Professionals certified according to UNI technical standards.

Given that there are no registers for professional figures in the experiential tourism area, and considering the European trend of not encouraging the creation of new national registers due to the difficulties of recognition at European level, the only options available for the recognition of professional requirements, in compliance with current legislation, they are the certification according to Law 4/2013 or the UNI certification.

Certification or Attestation of Quality and Professional Qualification of Services?

Certification is not easily an option, at least in Italy, unless assigned after a step leading to the definition of technical standards issued by the Italian National Unification Body (UNI). Such a standard could also be implemented by the European Standardization Body (EN) and ultimately by the International Organization for Standardization (ISO).

To understand the meaning of the various acronyms, just think that the international technical standard on quality management systems UNI EN ISO 9001 was issued at an international level (ISO) and implemented both at a European level (EN) and by the Italian national body of unification (UNI)

The proposed step, at least at a national level, is the following:

- First step: recognition by Associations authorized by the Ministry of Business and Made in Italy (formerly MISE) according to a scheme that is as close as possible in line with the provisions of the European EQF and ECVET standards and the ANPR UNI standard;
- Second step: transition to UNI personnel certification standards.

Currently, a first significant step in this direction has been taken in Italy. The **Italian Association of Tourism Professionals and Cultural Operators** (AIPTOC), which is included in the lists of the former MISE in accordance with Law 4/2013 and authorized to issue certificates of Quality and Professional Qualification of services according to the same law, has developed a scheme for the recognition of professional figures operating in the experiential sector. This scheme is in compliance with the reference Framework of the skills required and applied in the Tourism, Arts and Cultural Heritage sector, called Tourism, Arts, Heritage Competence Framework (TAH-CF).

5.2 Tourism, Arts, Heritage Competence Framework

For further information on the topic covered in this chapter, I refer you to another work of mine of which I report here only the essential elements[13].

5.2.1 Training Standards and Professional Standards

A classification of reference standards for professional qualifications and non-formal and informal training has historically been based on two approaches:

- **Professional Standards** (or employment standards). Based on the logic of employment (tasks, tasks and results obtained in the employment context. In essence: "what I am able to do in the workplace"
- **Educational Standards** (or education/training). Based on the logic of education and training (what you learn, how you learn and how you evaluate what you learn)

The need to integrate the two types of standards has been felt for years, as they are essentially not separate entities (world of education and work); this has meant that training standards have undergone a conceptual evolution over the years that allows this integration.

Educational standards are traditionally formulated in terms of **learning inputs**: disciplines, training contents, study program, training delivery methods, etc.); they have evolved to focus on **learning outcomes**. The latter are obtained at the end of the learning path and are expressed in terms of **Knowledge, Skills, Responsibility** and **Autonomy**. Therefore, the emphasis is no longer placed so much on the structure of a training course necessary to obtain a qualification, but rather on what an individual will be able to do after completing the training course.

[13] Ignazio Caloggero: "Turismo, Arte e Patrimonio Culturale: Profili Professionali e Nuovo Quadro delle Competenze Edizioni Centro Studi Helios (2022) ISBN: 9788832060171

The result of integration, facilitated by the latest European standards, such as EQF and ECVET, is the obtaining of standards associated with learning (whether formal, non-formal or informal) formulated in terms of Knowledge, Skills, and Autonomy and Responsibilities (regarding professional standards) and learning outcomes (regarding training standards).

5.2.2 The Tourism, Arts, Heritage Competence Framework (TAH-CF)

The Framework of reference of the skills required and applied in the **Tourism, Arts and Cultural Heritage sector, called Tourism, Arts, Heritage Competence Framework** (TAH-CF) it is made up of required skills, with particular reference to intellectual and highly specialized professions in the reference areas.

The skills (ability to **use knowledge** and **know-how**) constitute a combinatorial element that takes into account the **knowledge and personal abilities**, and the relative degree of autonomy and responsibility needed to solve a problem or carry out a **task**, even a complex one.

The skills, once the associated task has been specified, they are defined through the following components:

- Additional required knowledge
- Skills
- Level of Autonomy and Responsibility: required level of ability to apply knowledge and skills autonomously and responsibly. This level is associated with one of the eight levels referred to in the NQF/EQF classification.

The level of **Autonomy and Responsibility** of NQF/EQF correspondence should be associated for each individual competence.

Sometimes, the difference between one professional profile and another is precisely in the different level required for the individual skills; in fact, the same or similar skills can be associated with different EQF levels, depending on the importance they have in the specific professionalism.

In general, with the exception of some professional figures outlined in the e-CF, this does not occur, as an overall NQF/EQF level is attributed to the professional figure as a whole.

This practice occurs to simplify and provide a single EQF value, and it is possible thanks to the application of the 'qualitative principle of prevalence'.

The principle of prevalence is also cited in Annex 2, "Minimum criteria for the referencing of Italian qualifications to the National Qualifications Framework", of the MLPS - MIUR Decree 08/01/2018, "Establishment of the national qualifications framework issued within of the National Skills Certification System" pursuant to Legislative Decree 16 January 2013, n. 13.

«In the event that the qualification presents skills with different levels or different levels with respect to the dimensions or descriptions of the NQF and in any case, in the more comprehensive process of comparative and coherence assessments referred to in this point, the referencing must always take place on the basis of the qualitative principle of prevalence, attributing the most recurring level to the qualification.».

The TAH-CF has been implemented in accordance with the European Qualification Framework (EQF) and Recommendation 2009/C 155/02 (European Credit System for Vocational Education and Training - ECVET).

Two related reference standards are associated with the TAH-CF Framework:

- **SP/TAH-CF**: This is the **Professional Standard (SP)**, used to create or redefine professional profiles based on the TAH-CF framework and applicable to unregulated professions in the tourism, Arts and Entertainment, and Cultural Heritage sectors. Although focused on these areas, the scheme, at least in its basic guidelines, can also be used for other professions.
- **SF/TAH-CF:** This is the **Training Standard (SF)**, used to describe training courses based on the TAH-CF framework, but which can be applied to any training course relating to Formal and Non-Formal Learning.

The TAH-CF framework is constantly evolving, and an updated version can be viewed at the following web address for details:

https://www.turismoartiespettacolo.it/quadro-delle-competenze-del-turismo-delle-arti-e-del-patrimonio-culturale/

5.3 The Professionals of Experiential Experiences

The phenomenon of the **Experiential Transition** poses the need to develop new professional skills to manage the change triggered by the emerging experience economy. The new professional figures can be categorized based on the type of approach and the skills necessary to carry out their professional activities.

In the following list, a list of emerging professions. Each profession is associated with its corresponding EQF (European Qualifications Framework) level:

1) Mainly Corporate Approach

- **Specialist of Experiential Offers** (business approach): Professional already operating in their sector of expertise, with specialization in Experiential Offers. EQF level: 4
- **Experience Manager** (company approach): Professional who, generally within the company, fully manages the Experiential Offers, dealing with all its aspects, both operational and managerial. EQF level: 5
- **Experience Consultant** (company-oriented approach): Professional who, usually working externally to the company, provides consultancy for the creation of experiential offers and for obtaining the Experiential Quality Mark ®. EQF level: 6

2) Approach mainly aimed at Cultural Heritage

- **Experiential Tourism Manager** (EQF level: 7)

3) Approach aimed at training

- **Experienced Trainer** (EQF level: 5 to 7)

5.3.1 Experiential Offerings Specialist

Taken from schematic SP/TAH-CF/PST34 Ver. 1.3

EQF level: Fourth EQF level

The profession

The **Experience Specialist** is a professional figure who has the skills to carry out specialist support activities in the planning, management and evaluation of the experiential offers in various areas in which those events are feasible. This figure has in-depth knowledge of experiential principles and the characteristics of experiential offerings.

The Experience Specialist usually works as an employee or collaborator within organizations that provide experiential offers.

In order to take into account the different specializations linked to the different areas to which the experiential offers are applicable, it's important to consider the different activities indicated in the Repertoire of Experiential Activities.

Note:

1. The professional who has the preparation to carry out the activities associated with any area in which experiential offers are offered is considered an Experience Specialist.
2. The various specializations are not to be considered distinct in an absolute sense or incompatible with each other, as they differ only in certain operational and sectoral aspects.
3. It is assumed that the various specialist figures have adequate knowledge of the area in which they intend to operate.

Fundamental tasks and specific activities

- T1: Provide specialist support for the design of experiential offers
- T2: Provide specialist support for the management of experiential offers
- T3: Provide specialist support for the evaluation and improvement of the quality of the experiential event

For a detailed description of the scheme, including the expected skills and knowledge and the profile evaluation criteria, please refer to the updated scheme, which can be consulted at the following web address:

https://www.itinerariesperienziali.it/specialista-delle-esperienze-pst34-requisiti/

5.3.2 Experience Manager

Taken from schematic SP/TAH-CF/PST1 Ver. 1.4

EQF level: Fifth EQF level

The profession

The **Experience Manager** is a professional figure, with a highly specialized content, who possesses specific skills to carry out the following activities: planning, implementation and management of Experiential Events in the various reference sectors for which it is possible to create experiential events.

The Experience Manager has a deep knowledge of the techniques and methodologies used in the experiential field and of their related area, to which the experiential offers refer.

This figure can carry out the activities both on his own (self-employed) as a consultant, and for other interested parties as Experience Manager of Experiential Events.

In order to take into account the different specializations linked to the different areas to which the experiential offers are applicable, the different activities indicated in the Repertoire of Experiential Activities.

Note:

- The professional who has the preparation to carry out the activities associated with any area in which experiential offers are proposed is considered an Experience Manager.
- The various specializations are not to be considered distinct in an absolute sense or incompatible with each other, as they differ only in certain operational and sectoral aspects.
- It is assumed that the various specialist figures have adequate knowledge of the area in which they intend to operate.

Fundamental tasks and specific activities

- T1: Evaluate the needs and expectations of the user of the experiences
- T2: Analyze the Reference Context
- T3: Designing the Experiential Event Management System (SGEE)
- T4: Manage and maintain the Experiential Event Management System (SGEE)
    - Activity: T4.1: Plan activities from a qualitative and operational point of view
    - Activity: T4.2: Define internal procedures and regulations
    - Activity: T4.3: Coordinate human resources (staff)
    - Activity: T4.4: Ensure the correct execution of the experiential event
    - Activity: T4.5: Monitor the quality of the experiential event
    - Activity: T4.6: Improving the experiential event

For a detailed description of the scheme, including the skills and knowledge required and the profile evaluation criteria, please refer to the updated scheme, which can be consulted at the following web address:

https://www.itinerariesperienziali.it/responsabile-delle-esperienze/

5.3.3 Experiential Consultant

Taken from schematic SP/TAH-CF/PST32 Ver. 1.2

EQF level: Sixth EQF level

The profession

The **Experiential Consultant** is a professional figure, with a highly specialized content, who possesses specific skills to carry out activities of:

- Analysis of the services provided and the reference context
- Evaluation of the applicability of Experiential Quality Factors
- Transformation of services into experiential offers
- Documentation of the Experiential Offers
- Evaluation of the Quality of Experiential Offers
- Improvement of the Quality of Experiential Offerings

The Experiential Consultant usually carries out activities as an Expert/Consultant in the various reference areas.

Based on the type of deepening of knowledge, he can operate in the following specialist areas:

- **Tourist area**: Consultant for Experiential Tourism
- **Commercial area**: Experiential Marketing Consultant

In order to take into account the different specializations linked to the different areas to which the experiential offers are applicable, the different activities indicated in the **Repertoire of Experiential Activities**.

Note:

- The professional who has the preparation to carry out the activities associated with any sector in which experiential offers are proposed is considered an Experiential Consultant.
- The various specializations are not to be considered distinct in an absolute sense or incompatible with each other, as they differ only in certain operational and sectoral aspects.
- It is assumed that the various specialist figures have adequate knowledge of the sector in which they intend to operate.

Fundamental tasks and specific activities

- T1: Analyze the Reference Context
- T2: Evaluate the application of Experiential Quality Factors and transform services into Experiential Offers
- T3: Documenting Experiential Offerings
- T4: Evaluation of the Quality of Experiential Offerings

For a detailed description of the scheme, including the skills and knowledge required and the profile evaluation criteria, please refer to the updated scheme, which can be consulted at the following web address:

https://www.itinerariesperienziali.it/consulente-per-la-qualita-esperienziale-pst32-requisiti/

5.3.4 Experiential Tourism Manager

Taken from diagram SP/TAH-CF/PTUMN3 (Version 1.1)

EQF level: Seventh EQF level

The profession

The **Experiential Tourism Manager** is a professional figure, with a high intellectual content, who possesses specific skills to carry out activities of: conception, planning, communication, implementation, improvement and innovation regarding experiential offers.

The Experiential Tourism Manager has a profound knowledge of Cultural Heritage (tangible and immaterial), of the very concept of an experiential offer and of the knowledge necessary to conceive, plan, implement and manage, even independently, an experiential offer. It manages to reconcile knowledge of Cultural Tourism, and especially of Experiential Tourism, with specific paths of unique experiences, based on human relationships, which allow us to deepen our knowledge of elements of local identity as well as acquire multisensory experiences, also through direct participation in activities that constitute the experiential offer itself.

The Experiential Tourism Manager can carry out activities both on his own (self-employed) and for other interested parties as an Expert/Consultant.

In order to take into account the different specializations operating in the experiential area, and the correct assignment of skills, knowledge and competence, four specialist profiles are taken into consideration for the purposes of exercising the profession of Experiential Operator:

- **Profile P1**: Naturalistic Area
- **Profile P2**: Food and Wine Area
- **Profile P3**: Artistic Area (also including the Made in Italy sector linked to tourism - Artistic Craftsmanship)

- **Profile P4**: Intangible and demo-ethno-anthropological area (including tourism relating to the Intangible Cultural Heritage sector - which also includes the Demo-ethno-anthropological Heritage - and all forms of cultural and emotional tourism not considered in profiles P1, P2, P3).

Note:

1. The professional who has the preparation to carry out the activities associated with at least one of the four profiles indicated is considered a Manager of Experiential Tourism.
2. The four profiles are not to be considered distinct in an absolute sense or incompatible with each other, as they differ only in certain operational and sectoral aspects.
3. An Experiential Tourism Manager works in one or more of the areas indicated.
4. The professionals belonging to the P3 Profile are normally Artists and Artisans who intend to enhance and promote their art through experiences. It is assumed that these figures already have the knowledge, skills and competences necessary to carry out the profession in the artistic and/or artistic crafts field.

Fundamental tasks and specific activities

When assigning tasks, the following distinction was made:

- **Fundamental tasks**: essential tasks for all specialist profiles
- **Optional tasks**: additional tasks to the fundamentals that are at the discretion of the individual Experiential Operator

The individual tasks can possibly be described by a set of specific activities associated with them.

The specific tasks and activities are listed below, associating the knowledge, skills and competence requirements for each specific task or activity.

Fundamental tasks and specific activities for all specialist profiles

- T1: Assess tourism needs and expectations (tourism demand).
- T2: Analyzing the context of the tourism offer.
  - T2.1 Identify and analyze sector legislation.
  - T2.2 Identify and analyze the stakeholders (who are the interested parties: internal/external).
  - T3.3 Locate and Analyze attractions (Tourism Heritage).
- T3: Analyze costs and benefits and perform risk analysis (Risk Management).
- T4: Designing the experiential tourist offer.
- T5: Communicate the experiential tourist offer.
- T6: Realize the experiential offer.
  - T6.1: Plan activities from a qualitative and operational point of view.
  - T6.2: Define internal procedures and regulations.
  - T6.3: Managing economic resources (budget).
  - T6.4: Coordinate human resources (staff).
  - T6.5: Ensure the correct execution of the experiential offer.
  - T6.6: Verify and check compliance with applicable current legislation.
  - T6.7: Monitor the quality of the tourist offer.
- T7: Improving the tourist offer (continuous improvement)
- T8: Evaluate experiential offerings
- T9: Innovate experiential offerings

Optional tasks for all specialist profiles

- T10: Creating, Curating experiential exhibition events
- T11: Conduct Training on Experiential Tourism
- T12: Interfacing in a foreign language according to the territorial target of reference of its customers

For a detailed description of the scheme, including the skills and knowledge required and the profile evaluation criteria, please refer to the updated scheme, which can be consulted at the following web address:

https://www.itinerariesperienziali.it/regista-di-esperienze-manager-del-turismo-esperienziale-ptumn3-requisiti/

5.3.5 Cultural Heritage Interpreter

Taken from the SP/TAH-CF/PPC14 scheme (Version 1.3)

EQF level: Seventh EQF level

The profession

The **Heritage Interpreter** is a professional figure with a high intellectual content who has specific skills to carry out activities of:

- conception, planning, implementation, participation, communication, evaluation, improvement and innovation related to interpretive services (mediated interpreting) and to the paths of interpreting experiences (direct interpreting).
- identification, cataloguing, knowledge, interpretation, documentation, conservation, protection, enhancement, inherent to cultural heritage.

The Heritage Interpreter has a profound knowledge of his territory and of the cultural heritage in its various forms, from the material one (historical-artistic cultural heritage, landscape and natural heritage) to the immaterial one (tradition, folklore, art, food and wine, typical craftsmanship, history and local traditions), in order to identify and prepare, in a systemic way, both interpretative services and unique paths of cultural interpretation experiences. Furthermore, the Cultural Heritage interpreter adopts a systemic approach which highlights, during the entire interpretative process, typical aspects of experiential learning: motivation, interpersonal relationships, multisensoriality, local identities, centrality and uniqueness of the participants and originality of the tools used.

Note:

- **Interpretation services (indirect interpretation)**: creation of communication tools and services (signs, signs, maps, illustrative brochures, guides, flyers, multimedia productions and stations, displays, websites, apps, etc.) and design of interpretation paths and local development plans based on interpretation.
- **Interpretation Experience Paths (direct interpretation)**: initiatives that provide for the direct participation of both interpreters and guests in the interpretative activities.

In order to take into account the different specializations operating in the interpretation area and the correct assignment of skills, knowledge and competence, four specialist profiles are taken into consideration for the purposes of exercising the profession of Cultural Heritage Interpreter:

- **PPC14/P1**: Interpreter of the archaeological heritage
- **PPC14/P2**: Interpreter of the historic-artistic heritage
- **PPC14/P3**: Interpreter of the demo-ethno-anthropological heritage
- **PPC14/P4**: Interpreter of environmental heritage

Note:

1. The difference between the various forms of Cultural Heritage Interpretation is linked exclusively to the degree of sectoral specialization and the tools used during the entire interpretation process, as each Interpreter must still have robust knowledge and skills in all sectors. Therefore, there will not be distinct professionalisms but a single professionalism (Cultural Heritage Interpreter), specialized in one or more sectors that are relevant to Cultural Heritage in the broadest sense of the term.
2. The professional who has the preparation to carry out the activities associated with at least one of the five profiles indicated is considered Cultural Heritage Interpreter.
3. A Cultural Heritage Interpreter works in one or more of the areas indicated.

The Heritage Interpreter can be an employee or a self-employed person who provides their services to specialized centers, museums, eco museums, local authorities, cultural associations, organizations managing cultural heritage. Its activity can take place both indoors (classrooms, laboratories, museums and eco museums), and outdoors in direct contact with places of interest for carrying out the experience of cultural interpretation.

Fundamental tasks and specific activities

When assigning tasks, the following distinction was made:

- **Fundamental tasks:** indispensable tasks for the professional figure
- **Optional tasks:** additional tasks to the core that are at the discretion of the individual practitioner

Individual tasks can possibly be described by a set of specific activities associated with them.

The specific tasks and activities are listed below, associating, for each specific task or activity, the requisites of knowledge, skills and autonomy and responsibility (competences).

Fundamental tasks and specific activities for all specialist profiles

- T1: Carry out study, research and analysis activities in the field of Heritage Interpretation and in related and connected disciplines
- T2: Identify, catalogue, analyze, interpret and document Cultural Heritage
- T3: Analyze the reference context
- T4: Evaluate the needs and expectations of real and potential users for the reference area
- T5: Identify the purpose, objectives and type of interpretation of the heritage interpretation experience path (characteristics of the service)

- T6: Design and implement Cultural Heritage Interpretation Experience courses (direct interpretation)
- T7: Designing and implementing Cultural Heritage Interpretive Services (indirect interpretation)
- T8: Communicate
- T9 Monitor and evaluate
- T10: Improve (continuous improvement)
- T11: Realize, curate exhibition events on cultural themes

Optional tasks

- T12: Interfacing in a foreign language according to the territorial reference target of its users

The skills of the T12 task can also be made available by other members of the team in charge of carrying out the interpretive experience path where the user's request so requires.

For a detailed description of the scheme, including the skills and knowledge required and the profile evaluation criteria, please refer to the updated scheme, which can be consulted at the following web address:

https://www.itinerariesperienziali.it/interprete-del-patrimonio-culturale-heritage-interpreter-ppc14-requisiti/

6. Multimedia Archives of Experiences

6.1 Web 3.0 Databases

Let's explore the characteristics of a multimedia archive based on web 3.0 technology to understand its functioning and application potential:

- **Multimedia**: cards containing text, images, audio and video, and therefore with the possibility of inserting also audio guides, video guides and further in-depth multimedia documents.
- **GeoWeb**: information on interactive georeferenced Google maps, localization and identification of the route to reach the property (where relevant). Some goods are also visible on Street view, therefore with a 360° view of the context in which the good is located.
- **Social Web**: interactive cards with the possibility of inserting reviews and experiences. voting, comments and sharing on various social networks.
- **Multi thematic and Multi territorial (multi-archive)**: the archive allows the visualization on web pages of individual thematic and/or territorial archives (integrated with each other). By assigning new categories and tags, it is possible to create an unlimited number of thematic and territorial sub-archives.
- **Advanced Search**: for keywords, phrases (full text), cities, places, positions or geographical areas chosen by the user, physical location of the user, categories, subcategories and tags.
- **WikiWeb**: possibility of autonomous management of the files by the authors or collaborators themselves.
- **Multilingual**: the innovative neural machine translation system is used.

Its multi-thematic and multi-territorial nature makes it extremely versatile, particularly useful for selecting specific themes and/or geographical areas, as is common in experiential offers.

To understand the concept of web 3.0, I present to you some descriptive videos available on YouTube that refer to the Heritage Archive, created by me, which contains assets of the tangible and intangible cultural heritage of Sicily and Malta. It is important to note that, despite the differences between experiential offerings and cultural goods, the functioning of the experience archive remains essentially the same.

Conoscere l'Archivio Heritage - Parte Prima: Significato di GeoWeb e SocialWeb.

https://www.youtube.com/watch?v=cLDdupSamD0

Conoscere l'Archivio Heritage - Parte Seconda: Multi tematico e territoriale

https://www.youtube.com/watch?v=Or_yxLu-eRs

6.2 The Multimedia Experience Database

Within the project 'Experiential Tourism and Interpretation of Cultural Heritage', I have activated a sub-project which involves the creation of three Databases relating to the Experiential and Cultural Heritage Interpretation area:

- **Database of Experiential Offers**: Experiential and Interpretation Offers of Cultural Heritage.
- **Professionals Database of Experiences**: containing professionals who work in various capacities in the Experiential field and in the Heritage Interpretation.
- **Database of Training Paths**: masters, professional courses, short refresher courses.

A distinctive feature of databases is their mutual integration. When they are fully operational, it will be possible, for example, to identify the professionals who possess specific skills or the training courses that provide these skills, starting from the skills themselves. Similarly, starting from the Repertoire of Experiential Activities, it will be possible to identify the experiential offers available.

Below are some links and related QR-codes for further information:

Experience databases

https://www.itinerariesperienziali.it/banche-dati-esperienziali/

Useful bibliography

- Charles Spence – Gastrophysics: the new science of eating – Readrink 2020 editions
- Quality, Operational Models and Competitiveness of the Tourist Offer by Ignazio Caloggero. Helios Study Center Editions 2019
- Ignazio Caloggero: Experiential Paths and Interpretation of Cultural Heritage Vol. 1: Origins and Theoretical Principles – Helios Study Center 2022
- Ignazio Caloggero: From Eco museums to Cultural Heritage Interpretation Experience Centers – Helios 2023 Study Center
- Ignazio Caloggero – Tourism, Art and Cultural Heritage: Professional Profiles and New Skills Framework – Helios Study Center Editions – Ragusa 2022
- Heritage Interpretation Centers: The Hicira Manual
- Freeman Tilden – Interpreting Our Heritage – 2019 English Edition – Geographic Library
- Franco Bianco: Introduction to hermeneutics - Laterza 1998
- Hugues De Varine: The singular and plural Eco Museum – Concrete Utopias -2021
- Directive 2005/36/EC of the European Parliament and of the Council of 7 September 2005 on the recognition of professional qualifications
- Directive 2013/55/EU of the European Parliament and of the Council amending Directive 2005/36/EC on the recognition of professional qualifications
- Council Recommendation on the European Qualifications Framework for lifelong learning of 22 May 2017 (European Qualification Framework – EQF), repealing the previous recommendation of 23 April 2008
- Recommendation of the European Parliament and of the Council of 18 June 2009 on the establishment of a European credit system for vocational education and training (ECVET) – (2009/C 155/02)
- Recommendation of the European Parliament and of the Council of 18 June 2009 on the establishment of a European Quality Assurance Reference Framework for Vocational Education and Training

- Council Recommendation of 20 December 2012 on the validation of non-formal and informal learning (2012/C 398/01)
- European guidelines for the validation of non-formal and informal learning – European Center for the Development of Vocational Training (CEDEFOP) – 2016
- Decree MLPS – MIUR 08/01/2018 "Establishment of the national framework of qualifications issued within the national system of certification of skills referred to in legislative decree 16 January 2013, n. 13"
- European Credit Transfer and Accumulation System (ECTS) User Guide, 2009)
- UNI 11697:2017: "Unregulated professional activities - Professional profiles relating to the processing and protection of personal data - Knowledge, skill and competence requirements"
- UNI 11506: Unregulated professional activities - Professional figures operating in the ICT sector - Requirements for the assessment and certification of knowledge, skills and competences for ICT professional profiles based on the e-CF model
- UNI 11621-1 "Methodology for the construction of professional profiles based on the e-CF system" in turn taken from the CWA 16458 prepared by the CEN Workshop Agreement. The model, although developed for ICT profiles, has the advantage that it can be applied in any area
- APNR Scheme (Unregulated Professional Activities) adopted by UNI for technical standardization in the APNR area
- CEN Guide 14 "Guidelines for standardization activities on the qualification of professions and personnel
- Bloom, BS (Ed.), Engelhart, MD, Furst, EJ, Hill, WH and Krathwohl, DR Taxonomy of Educational Objectives: Handbook 1: Cognitive Domain. (1956)
- Anderson, LW, Krathwohl, DR (Eds.) A Taxonomy for Learning, Teaching and Assessing. A Revision of Bloom's Taxonomy of Educational Objectives. (2001)
- B. Joseph Pine, James H. Gilmore: The Experience Economy. Beyond the service – Etas 2000, Rizzoli 2013
- Bernd H. Schmitt: Experiential Marketing. The Free Press New York-1999

- David Allen Kolb: Experiential learning: experience as the source of learning and development – New Jersey 1984
- Charles Spence – Gastrophysics. The new science of eating, p. 22
- Charles Spence – Gastrophysics. The new science of eating, p. 18
- Charles Spence – Gastrophysics. The new science of eating, p. 99
- Charles Spence – Gastrophysics. The new science of eating
- Freeman Tilden – Interpreting our Heritage chap. 10: "Nothing in excess"
- Ignazio Caloggero – Experiential Paths and Interpretation of Cultural Heritage Vol. 1: Origins and Theoretical Principles – Helios Study Center 2022
- Freeman Tilden: Interpreting our heritage – 2019 Italian edition – Geographical Library p. 29
- https://www.heritagedestination.com/hdc-training—what-is-heritage-interpretation
- Regarding the need for self-realization, see Abraham H. Maslow's scale of needs
- Ignazio Caloggero – Quality, Operating Models and Competitiveness of the Tourist Offer. ISBN: 9788894321906 – 2017
- The six-step technique is inspired by the CiVIT resolution n. 88/2010 and by some principles indicated by the general reference scheme of the charter of public health services (DPCM 19 May 1995). I adapted the proposed methodology to the case of cultural offers and tourist services in general.
- Ignazio Caloggero: "Tourism, Art and Cultural Heritage: Professional Profiles and New Framework of Competencies Editions Helios Study Center (2022) ISBN: 9788832060171

www.ingramcontent.com/pod-product-compliance
Lightning Source LLC
LaVergne TN
LVHW080451160826
845677LV00006B/1337

* 9 7 8 8 8 3 2 0 6 0 2 8 7 *